THREADING THE GENERATIONS

Mary Shaifer, A. K. Shaifer's granddaughter, c. 1870, at about nine years of age, standing next to table over which a quilt is draped.

Threading the Generations

A Mississippi Family's Quilt Legacy

Mary Elizabeth Johnson
and Carol Vickers

Photography by J. D. Schwalm

Historic photographs from the collection of Elizabeth Shaifer Hollingsworth

For Elizabeth Smith
with all good wishes,
Carol Vickers
Feb. '08

Bobbye Hollingsworth

UNIVERSITY PRESS OF MISSISSIPPI JACKSON

www.upress.state.ms.us

The University Press of Mississippi is a member of the Association of American University Presses.

Elizabeth Shaifer Hollingsworth wishes to acknowledge L & L Photography of Vicksburg, Mississippi, for their excellent service in duplicating the historic photographs included in this book.

Library of Congress Cataloging-in-Publication Data
Johnson, Mary Elizabeth.
Threading the generations : a Mississippi family's quilt legacy : historic photos from the collection of Elizabeth Shaifer Hollingsworth / Mary Elizabeth Johnson and Carol Vickers ; photography by J. D. Schwalm.
   p. cm.
Includes bibliographical references and index.
ISBN 1-57806-745-6 (cloth : alk. paper)
1. Quilting—Mississippi—Port Gibson—History—19th century. 2. Quilting—Mississippi—Port Gibson—History—20th century. 3. Hollingsworth, Elizabeth Shaifer—Art collections. I. Vickers, Carol. II. Hollingsworth, Elizabeth Shaifer. III. Title.
TT835.J5855 2005
746.46'0922762'285—dc22   2004018592

British Library Cataloging-in-Publication Data available

CONTENTS

INTRODUCTION 7

CHAPTER ONE

The Back Story: How the First Shaifer Got to Mississippi 13

CHAPTER TWO

The Battle of Port Gibson: The Shaifer Women Make History 23

CHAPTER THREE

After the War 31

CHAPTER FOUR

Unique New Friendships 44

CHAPTER FIVE

Mother and Daughter: "Lizzie" and "Dear Laura" 53

CHAPTER SIX

Into the Twenty-First Century: New Talent Joins the Shaifers 87

NOTES 111

BIBLIOGRAPHY 114

INDEX 116

INTRODUCTION

THE HORSE SHIED at a sound in the deep woods off to the left, toward the river. It was almost as though he knew that he was on the notorious Natchez Trace, where highwaymen, thieves, smugglers, and other unsavory characters lay in wait for the unwary traveler; he was more suspicious than usual. His rider, Abram Keller Shaifer, patted his neck and made soothing clucking sounds. "Whoa, boy, that's okay. It's just a tree limb falling."

A. K. resettled himself uncomfortably in the saddle. His rheumatism was working on him again. How could he withstand a trip on horseback all the way to Nashville, especially since he was now only a little north of Natchez? The lap of the journey from New Orleans to Natchez had not been so bad, but the longer he rode, the more his hip joints hurt. "Not fair for a man of my age to be so afflicted," muttered A. K. to himself.

The year was 1813, and Abram Keller Shaifer was thirty years old and a remarkably prescient businessman—he seemed gifted with foresight for good deals. A. K. had a knack for figuring out where to apply his efforts so they would pay off handsomely; his track record as he moved from Fredericktown, Maryland, to Philadelphia to the wilds of Tennessee bore witness to his prodigious talents for making gold out of dross—until now.

His most recent undertaking had not turned out well, because of the impossibility of being in two places at once. He had traveled hard from Nashville to New Orleans, and now he was headed back home, having made barely enough on this latest venture to cover expenses. But even if the amount of money had been a hundred times more, it could not have salved the pain of his rheumatoid arthritis. "I think I'll stop in and see those folks near Fayette that were so kind to me on the way down," A. K. decided. "I'll feel better if I give this hip some rest."

Thus it was that the first Shaifer made his way to what is now Port Gibson, one of the oldest towns in Mississippi, situated about halfway between Natchez and present-day Vicksburg. A. K. Shaifer paid a visit to his friends, and he never went home to east Tennessee. Instead, he settled on what was, at that time, the frontier of America. The story of the family he founded there gives intimate glimpses into the normal, everyday life of that time and place. As we follow A. K.'s descendents, we celebrate their accomplishments, both great and small, and rejoice with them that the family commitment to the civic good has remained a tradition throughout the generations.

The history of the Shaifers is not just a paper trail, and that is what makes it so accessible. We can still travel the road from Port Gibson to the original home place a little bit west, at Holly Hill; we can visit the Shaifer house where the Battle of Port Gibson began; we can see the quilts that generations of Shaifer women have stitched. These things have not vanished—they are here to rekindle our imaginations.

It is clear that the family from whom A. K. chose his bride (as well as other families who became part of the Shaifer ancestry) brought quilts with them into south Mississippi in the late eighteenth century, and that Shaifer women went about making quilts as a normal facet of everyday life, generation after generation, up to the present. Libby Shaifer Hollingsworth, the current caretaker of her family's amazing repository of quilts, has said that, as she was growing up, quilts were as common as furniture in their home.

"Chests were full of them; beds were stacked with them. We just lived with them. Actually, we didn't consider them anything special," says Mrs. Hollingsworth, indicating that quilts were, to her family, just part of a well-outfitted household. One wouldn't dream of attempting to keep house without quilts, and the making of them was simply taken for granted as part of the yearly cycle of provisioning and replenishing necessary household items.

Echoing a reaction expressed by perhaps thousands of quilt owners across the country upon attending a quilt documentation day, Mrs. Hollingsworth continues, "I didn't realize how unique my quilt collection is until I attended the Port Gibson quilt-sharing day [held by the Mississippi Quilt Association on November 2, 1996]. I took five quilts, which was the limit. It was a slow day, so I took five more, then five more. By the time the quilt-sharing day was over, I had taken twenty-nine quilts to be documented."

Those twenty-nine quilts are about half the total collection of family

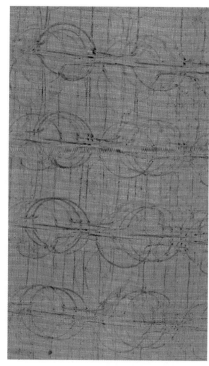

I.1. Throughout the years, the Shaifer quilts have been stored in various ways and in various places: this one shows the rusty imprints of iron bedsprings, indicating that it spent some time beneath a mattress before the invention of box springs.

quilts. The count was originally established at fifty, but occasionally another quilt will surface, as some long-packed box in the attic of the current Shaifer home is opened. (All the quilts currently known to exist are presented on these pages.)

As astonishing as this collection of quilts is for its breadth and beauty, it becomes even more fascinating as its background is revealed. The quilts bind together five generations of one family—they are the common thread picked up and passed along from one woman to the next. And, just as the Shaifer quilts have provided the portal for looking back into this family history, so can any family's quilts provide clues to the family's collective past.

We, the authors and Libby Hollingsworth, hope that readers will become inspired to let their own quilts lead them deeper into their own personal histories. We further hope that this story of one collection of quilts will not only appeal to those who stitch their own designs, but be a comfort to, and inspiration for, those who do not make quilts themselves, but love them, buy them, take care of them, show them, and read about them. It is a reward in itself to be a caretaker of the past.

THREADING THE GENERATIONS

CHAPTER ONE

The Back Story: How the First Shaifer Got to Mississippi

The first of the American family that became known as Shaifer was Henry Schaeffer, who immigrated to America in 1774. Although he was born in Lorraine, France, he was living in Berne, Switzerland, in 1774. Henry and his wife, Elizabeth Keller Schaeffer, settled quickly in Fredericktown, Maryland. It was soon after arriving there on October 9, 1774, that a son, Abram Keller, was born. Other children had preceded him, but our story concerns the history of this first American child and the youngest of the children.

Much is known of Abram's life, thanks to the recollections set down by his son. In 1895, A. K. Shaifer Jr. wrote many of the stories about his father's past that the family had enjoyed telling and retelling.

He left his boyhood home so young that he did not have a chance to learn and remember very much of his own people. When he arrived at school age, his parents proposed to send him to a Dutch [Pennsylvania German] school, but, like all young Americans, he protested seriously. His parents seemed to think nothing of the protests, but when the time for him to start to school had nearly arrived, young Abram was missing.

The next we hear of him, he was bound as an apprentice to a hatter in the city of Philadelphia. No doubt he was a gay youth, as he later spoke of having organized an association to correct the dress, etc., of the young gentlemen of the shop. One stringent regulation was always enforced by fine or otherwise: every workman entering the shop must have his hair dressed in the highest style of "puff and powder" with [his clothing appropriate to] puff and powder style.[1]

A slightly different version of this history is provided by a great-grandson of Abram's, who wrote the following in 1935:

Henry Schaeffer's will provided that Abram Keller was to be sent to school and educated. [This probably meant that Abram was to be sent to college. He had undoubtedly attended local elementary and primary schools throughout his childhood and youth.] Instead, he was kept on the farm, doing chores, driving the cows home, etc. He was not allowed to go to school. One time, after starting after the cows, he never returned home. He apprenticed himself to a hatter, added the i to his name [and eliminated the c and an e and an f], and started a new dynasty.[2]

East Tennessee is where Abram next showed up, first working as an Indian trader at Tellie's Garrison. He must have been successful at merchandising because he soon opened a store of his own. A favorite family legend claims that one of Abram's employees was fourteen-year-old Sam

Houston, who quickly discovered that he was not cut out for retail. Clerking in a store did not suit him, as he told his employer, "I would rather measure deer tracks than tape, and I am going to the woods."[3] This is the same Sam Houston who proved to be not only an excellent woodsman, but a heroic fighter at the defense of the Alamo.

It soon came to the attention of the business-minded Abram that innovative entrepreneurs were shipping flatboats loaded with merchandise from the Tennessee River down the Ohio and Mississippi Rivers. Although the majority of the flatboats were loaded with bulk commodities, some of them functioned as floating merchants. Such boats periodically pulled into the riverbank, and their enterprising captains sold such items as flour, millstones, iron, and perhaps "Monongahela whisky,"[4] to those who congregated at the stopping points. Eventually the boatmen made their way to New Orleans, where they sold off piecemeal whatever remained of their inventory. Those with bulk commodities found factors, or agents, awaiting them at the docks, anxious to buy the entire boatload of timber, cotton, or whatever—at significantly lower prices than the cargo would command when the factors resold it. An alternative to this arrangement, more suitable for a long-term relationship between supplier and factor, was the commission agent, who arranged the sale of the cargo and took his payment as a percentage of the price he was able to secure for the product.

With no power source of their own, flatboats could travel downriver by riding on the currents, but were no good for a return trip up the river against the currents; consequently, they were sold for lumber at their final destination.[5] The erstwhile boatmen had to turn into woodsmen in order to return to their homes; they walked overland up the fabled Natchez Trace through Mississippi to Nashville, and from there to other points north and eastward.

This river-powered method of trading seemed to Abram to be an opportunity too good to miss, so he, according to A. K. Jr.'s narrative,

> decided to speculate in tobacco. He commenced gathering the tobacco, and as fast as he could load a boat, he started it down the river to his commission merchant in New Orleans. He continued this until he had shipped the seventh flatboat load of tobacco, then he took a horse to go through by land [by going south on the Natchez Trace] and meet his boats in New Orleans.
>
> Unfortunately, he was attacked so severely by rheumatism on the journey that he had to take to bed in Fayette, Mississippi [in Jefferson County]. As soon as he had recovered sufficiently, he hurried to New Orleans, where, to his distress, he discovered that his commission merchant had gone into bankruptcy. However, the seventh load of tobacco arrived shortly after Abram did, and, with the greatest difficulty, he managed to take possession of it. . . . [T]he other six loads of tobacco went entirely into the hands of the commissioners.[6]

This unlucky enterprise appears to have been one of the few attempted by Abram Shaifer that did not immediately advance his fortunes. However, the calamity indirectly influenced his decision to change his life once again.

As he traveled north from New Orleans on the Natchez Trace, Abram decided to stop a while in Fayette, Mississippi, no doubt to visit again with the kind friends who had taken such good care of him on his trip down from Tennessee. His visit turned into a lengthy one, with Abram taking a job running a store, which he eventually owned. Because early stores usually functioned more or less as the community center, Abram was in a perfect situation to hear all the local news and to get to know his neighbors for miles around.

Included in Abram's general neighborhood was Grindstone Ford, a small, active settlement located where the Natchez Trace crossed Bayou Pierre. It was at Grindstone Ford that Abram came to know the George Wilson Humphreys family, who had settled in Claiborne County in 1789. Captain Humphreys' daughter, Elizabeth Hannah, known as Betsey, became Abram's bride on May 15, 1817. (Betsey's grandfather was General Ralph Humphreys, a hero of the Revolutionary War.) The Humphreys must have taken Abram into the heart of the family because one of his and Betsey's grandchildren commented, "After their marriage, Abram seemed never to have had a desire to return to see any of his relatives in Maryland."[7]

The town of Port Gibson was just beginning to establish itself, and, by the time of his marriage, Abram had already set up a business in the center of town near the courthouse. Records show that he had purchased a commercial building there by 1815. A. K. Jr.'s story continues:

After he became well known, Abram was elected tax collector of Claiborne County. Tax collecting was not the easy, safe business then that it is now. The collector was also the assessor, and consequently had to see every man in the county twice in the year. Because this kept him busy most of the time, he sold his store and bought a place out from town. He purchased

1.1. Abram Keller "A. K." Shaifer, born October 9, 1774, in Fredericktown, Maryland, and died April 26, 1860, in Claiborne County, Mississippi. He was the founding father of the Mississippi Shaifers.

1.2. Elizabeth Hannah "Betsey" Humphreys Shaifer, born April 9, 1798, in Claiborne County, Mississippi, and died October 25, 1867, in Claiborne County, Mississippi. She was the wife of A. K. Shaifer; she listed four "comforts" in her will.

some slaves as well. [This account also records that the couple had been given slaves as a wedding gift from the bride's father.]

Father held the office of assessor and collector for four years, and then he decided to stand for a more lucrative position. Accordingly, he ran for and obtained the office of sheriff of Claiborne County. He held the sheriff's office for eight years, after which he refused to canvass again.

Father was a devoted Mason, belonging to Washington Lodge, Port Gibson. He was often a delegate to the grand bodies of Tennessee and Mississippi; in fact, he acted as Grand Master of the first Grand Lodge of Tennessee, after the utter failure of both the Grand Master and the Grand Senior Warden.[8]

Abram was a man of energy and outgoing personality and was very aware of his civic responsibility; from an early age, he was an organizer, as evidenced by his experience in the Pennsylvania haberdashery. In 1818, he helped organize the first public library in the state: it was originally named the Literary and Library Company of Gibson's Port. (The town began as Gibson's Landing, then was named Gibson's Port, then finally became Port Gibson.) Abram was chosen as one of six selectmen (plus a president) when Port Gibson was incorporated on February 9, 1821, under Mississippi state law.

The marriage of Abram and Betsey Shaifer resulted in the birth of eight children, six of whom lived to adulthood. Most of the children were born in the town of Port Gibson, in a rented brick house "behind where the Musgroves of Church Street now live" (known to locals as "Miss Phoebe's"), according to an early account.[9] In the meantime, around 1826 to 1828, Abram began building a home at the plantation, "Holly Hill," about four miles toward the river, west of Port Gibson. Perhaps because he was anxious to be living on his own property, or because he knew that the grand house he planned as the permanent family residence would take years to complete, Abram decided to first build a smaller house located somewhat apart from where the mansion would be; he planned the smaller house to become the residence for the plantation overseer.

The home, made of cypress and still standing, consists of four rooms downstairs, two bedrooms upstairs, and a dining room and kitchen off the back of the house. Also on the property were a barn, chicken house, smokehouse, gin, press, mill, and living quarters for thirty to forty slaves. A neighbor's diary of the time describes the original Shaifer home as a small white house covered with grapevines. Abram moved Betsey and their children to Holly Hill in the late 1820s. In 1833, Abram Keller Shaifer Jr., the fourth son and last child, was born.

1.3. The A. K. Shaifer house at Holly Hill, which today belongs to the state of Mississippi, given by his descendants in 1979 and placed under the jurisdiction of Mississippi Department of Archives and History in 2002.

There is reason to believe that Betsey Shaifer furnished both the brick rental home in Port Gibson and the dwelling at Holly Hill with quilts. In her will, probated in Claiborne County on December 24, 1867, there are listed—among the "2 feather beds" valued at $20, the "mattress and bolster" worth $10, the "shuck mattress" at $2.50, the "moss mattress" at $5, the "5 counterpains" and other bedding—"4 comforts," valued at a total of $6.00. "Comforts" was a term commonly used at that time for quilts.

If the Humphreys brought quilts when they moved from Virginia, it can be assumed that they would have been representative of quilts to be found in a well-to-do Mississippi household of the first half of the nineteenth century. (See *Mississippi Quilts* for a thorough discussion of quilt styles of this period.[10]) It will remain a mystery as to whether these were of whole-cloth toile, carefully stitched chintz *broderie perse,* or white work with its classic motifs of pineapples and feathered plumes, or whether they were examples of the amazing artistry that could be accomplished with many-hued and many-shaped patchwork pieces. What *is* certain is that the very first family of Shaifers in Port Gibson, Mississippi, had, at the very least, four quilts in their home.[11] There were probably additional household quilts; the four listed in the will could well have been part of a set of complete bed hangings, and thereby more important and valuable. Less significant quilts would have been left out of the inventory as having little value.

Abram and Betsey Shaifer lived out their lives at Holly Hill. Rather than following the path chosen by his neighbors, who raised cotton exclusively, Abram elected to farm primarily produce, and this choice proved to be a good one. Although he did grow some cotton, his major products were corn, sweet potatoes, beans, peaches, and melons. There is evidence from family diaries that the west-side community, around Holly Hill, was the breadbasket of the area, and that the Shaifer family and their neighbors raised a majority of the fruit and vegetables for a large area of southwest Mississippi. The family prospered financially and by the outbreak of the Civil War was among the most prominent in the area.[12] Abram's uncanny ability to choose the right, though not necessarily traditional, course made him an almost visionary entrepreneur, and his decision to farm vegetables instead of cotton would prove to be a great benefit to his son and namesake.

Abram Shaifer died in April of 1860; Betsey followed him seven years later. One of Abram's grandchildren later recalled sitting at his knee when he was an old man busily involved in making a scrapbook for each of his grandchildren. (Two of the scrapbooks survive today.) This grandchild, born in 1846, described Abram as "still maintaining a style of dress of knee breeches, shoes with silver buckles, and a circular cape."[13]

CHAPTER TWO

The Battle of Port Gibson:
The Shaifer Women Make History

The children of Abram and Betsey Shaifer included two daughters born eight years apart, one who lived to only five years of age and the other who died at the age of fourteen, and a third daughter who lived to the age of twenty-five before succumbing to yellow fever during the 1855 epidemic. A fourth daughter married a man who owned a plantation but was primarily engaged in the mercantile business in Port Gibson and New Orleans. She lived out a full seventy-six years, the only one of the daughters to reach old age.

All four of the Shaifer sons reached maturity. The oldest moved to "Claranook" plantation in Tensas Parish, Louisiana, after he married; he went on to be a part of the Confederate secret service, helping to move dispatches back and forth across the Mississippi River during the War between the States. The second son lived at Holly Hill, but spent much of his life as a soldier, serving in the Mexican-American War under Colonel Jefferson Davis and in the Army of Northern Virginia during the Civil War. The third son, nicknamed "Pill" because of his middle name of Pilsworth, practiced medicine in Claiborne County, becoming fondly known far and wide as "Dr. Pill." Upon marrying an only child of wealthy parents, he gave up his medical practice, although still a young man, and devoted himself to managing the properties left to his wife by her parents. Among those properties was "Edgehill," a home near Port Gibson, which is glowingly described in a Shaifer family document:

> In 1863, Edgehill had well-kept lawns covered with forest trees which encircled the house. . . . There were flowerbeds that were a blaze of color, with roses, jessamine, verbenas, and old-fashioned flowers. . . . They lived like nabobs and drove fine horses. . . .
>
> Stephen Pilsworth Shaifer joined the Fairview Rifles, but his health did not allow him to remain. He returned to the plantation and ran it in the interests of the Army, taking care of the wounded, etc. He had plenty to do as a physician and surgeon. Unionists said he was running a "D—— Rebel hotel."[1]

The fourth son, Abram K. Shaifer Jr., was known to family and friends as "Kell." Born at Holly Hill, he lived all of his life there. He followed in the business his father had set up, that of growing fruits and vegetables for export around the country. When he was twenty-four years old, he married Elizabeth Chamberlain Girault, and with her had four sons, two of whom died in infancy.

Five years after his and Elizabeth's marriage, in January of 1862, Kell joined the 121st Mississippi Light Artillery, Confederate States of America. During the War between the States he traveled with his unit to different

2.1. Abram Keller "Kell" Shaifer Jr. in his Confederate States of America uniform. He is twenty-nine years old.

2.2. Elizabeth Girault Shaifer, wife of Kell Shaifer. Her health was destroyed as a result of the trauma of the Battle of Port Gibson.

postings as ordered (including Blakely, Alabama, on Mobile Bay, the scene of the last battle of the Civil War, which was fought on April 9, 1865). On the night of April 30, 1863, he was at Port Hudson, Louisiana (little knowing that within a month he would begin, along with sixty-eight hundred Confederate troops, one of the longest sieges in American military history—lasting forty-eight days and involving thousands of casualties).

At home at Holly Hill were his wife and two sons (Benjamin Humphreys, five years old, and A. K. III, three years old); his mother, Betsey Shaifer, who, at sixty-five years of age had been without her beloved husband, A. K. Sr., for three years and was in failing health; and his sister-in-law, whose husband was serving in the Army of Northern Virginia, along with her two children, Mary and George.

Elizabeth Girault Shaifer had the responsibility of caring for her mother-in-law, her sister-in-law, and four small children, plus managing the plantation with no men to help in the fields. She was also recovering from the loss of an infant son, George Girault Shaifer, who had died in January of 1863. The war was in full swing, every able-bodied man had been called into action, and General Ulysses S. Grant had been trying to take Vicksburg, thirty-five miles north, for months. Elizabeth was undoubtedly able to guess that Yankee troops were on the move when she observed, on the afternoon of April 30, that not only had a Confederate brigade been posted earlier that day at Magnolia Church, a short distance from Holly Hill, but a little outpost of soldiers was also stationed at her front gate. Besides, it was common knowledge that General Grant was considering invading Vicksburg from the south.

Grant had put his plan into action. He had moved twenty-four thousand Federal troops by boat down the Mississippi River to Bruinsburg, a few miles west of Holly Hill, and was marching them north. His strategy was to sneak up on Vicksburg, thirty-five miles north of Port Gibson, and surprise the besieged city by attacking from the land, rather than the river. But first he had to get through Claiborne County. The region abounded in hollows and ravines. These ravines were choked with underbrush and cane, while the ridges along which the roads ran were intensively cultivated. General Grant was quoted as saying, "[It was] the most broken land I have ever seen."[2]

One of Grant's soldiers later wrote about the march. His description of the road (the existence of which the Federals had learned about from a Louisiana slave[3]) is accurate today; if anything, the road, which winds between the high loess banks, has buried itself even deeper between those banks as the years have passed.

At 9 o'clock at night we start away and, climbing the steep hill, push on toward Port Gibson. As we pass along, an old darky gives his blessings, but fears there will be few of us to ever return. The moon is shining above us, and the road is romantic in the extreme. The artillery wagons rattle forward, and the heavy tramp of many men gives a dull but impressive sound. In many places, the road seems to end abruptly, but when we come to the place, we find it turning at right angles, passing through narrow valleys, sometimes through hills, and presenting the best opportunity to the Rebels for defense if they had but known our purpose.[4]

As the Federals were marching toward them, Confederate General Green decided about midnight to check on his pickets. As he rode up to Holly Hill, he found Elizabeth Girault Shaifer and the other two ladies

frantically piling their household effects on a wagon. Green assured the women that there was no need to hurry, since the Yankees couldn't possibly arrive before daybreak. Hardly had Green spoken before there was a crash of musketry—the pickets had exchanged shots with the Union vanguard.… The women leaped into the wagon and headed for Port Gibson, while General Green returned to Magnolia Church to alert his troops. The Confederate pickets fell back before the Federal advance. During the Battle of Port Gibson, the Shaifer house served as General John A. McClernand's General Head Quarters and a Union hospital.[5]

The Shaifer women fled the house in such haste that they had no opportunity to pack all their household items—they were concerned with saving

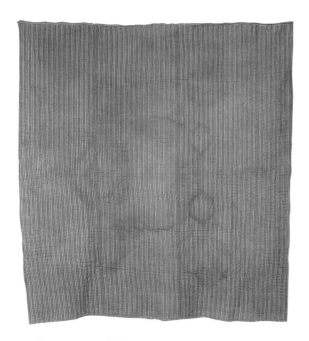

2.3. The mysterious whole-cloth quilt. The color that now appears as teal was probably originally green and was formed by dyeing yellow over blue, or blue over yellow. The yellow is gradually fading, or becoming what is known in quilt terminology as "fugitive."

their lives and the lives of their children—and they managed to load only a few valuables. During the time that the house was used as a headquarters of the Union general and the ten days or so that it was used as a hospital, everything in and around it was at the disposal of the occupying forces. Consequently, none of the bedding from that time or earlier survives. Quilts, sheets, blankets and other household linens were used to make bandages and bedding for the wounded.

However, there is one quilt of mysterious origin that has only recently been discovered; it has been packed away in the family attic for decades. It is a whole-cloth piece, and the fabric is of a teal, white, and pink stripe typical of the mid-nineteenth century. Intriguingly, a photograph in the Shaifer family album captures "Mammy Mary" (servant) wearing a dress of a nearly identical striped fabric. It is almost impossible to avoid speculation. Could it be that one Shaifer family quilt somehow made it through the war? Was it perhaps a quilt that Mammy Mary had made? Was the fabric in her portrait dress and the quilt the same? The answers to these questions will probably never be known for sure. We do know that Mammy Mary and two of her own children (Americus and Mary Ann) were with the Shaifer women that night and helped them load the wagon. Although many slaves left their white families at the beginning of the War, Mammy Mary chose to remain with the Shaifers throughout and after the war, and she became the one constant in little Ben and A. K.'s (III) lives for their first ten years.[6]

On May 1, 1863, General Grant's twenty-four thousand troops fought a Confederate force of eight thousand in the Battle of Port Gibson. It was the first victory of Grant's successful strategy to capture Vicksburg by attacking through the "back door." According to legend, Grant spared Port Gibson because it was "too beautiful to burn." No doubt the Presbyterian Church, whose steeple is capped with a ten-and-a-half-foot-tall golden hand pointing to heaven, contributed to his enchantment with the little town. The hand was originally put in place around 1860 to honor the church's pastor, a fiery orator named Zebulon Butler, who had a distinctive pulpit mannerism—"the upright and clenched hand, with the index finger pointing heavenward."[7] (The hand on the church today was made in 1901 of iron sheathed in gold leaf; weather and woodpeckers destroyed the original gold-painted wooden one.) Zebulon Butler was minister to Abram and Betsey Shaifer and their children and their families until both men's deaths in 1860.

The Shaifer women returned to Holly Hill soon after the Battle of Port Gibson. The house had bullet-ridden walls—the frame around the por-

2.4. Photograph of "Mammy Mary" (servant), in a photo album inscribed, "Presented to Amanda Guice by A. K. Shaifer before their marriage in 1865."

trait of Elizabeth Hannah (Betsey) Humphreys Shaifer still contains a minié ball shot into it from outside the house; the hole and the nail on which the portrait was hung remain as they were. The women found desolation: the house had been used as an amputation hospital and the floors were covered with blood; half-buried bodies were scattered throughout the grounds; all provisions had been used up or carried off; even the trees were destroyed. Confronting her home's awful devastation (and its subsequent cleanup) completely traumatized Elizabeth Girault Shaifer; she never recovered and after experiencing a very difficult pregnancy, she died on June 15, 1864, "as a result of the Battle of Magnolia Church."[8] The baby, a son named Edwin Thomas, died two days later.

CHAPTER THREE

After the War

When A. K. "Kell" Shaifer Jr., exhausted and recovering from several injuries, returned home to Holly Hill after the Battle of Blakely (fought on April 9, 1865), he found a shattered homestead and the graves of his wife and two of his sons. He immediately began to rebuild, and on November 28, 1865, married Amanda Caroline Guice. An accomplished cook and seamstress, she became Kell's dedicated companion and partner and the devoted mother of his two remaining sons, Benjamin Humphreys Shaifer and A. K. Shaifer III. The couple soon had a son of their own, Percy Leon Shaifer, born on October 15, 1866.

Right away Kell's attention turned to the restoration of the business he had conducted before the war, that of raising fruits and vegetables for export, continuing the tradition his father had established. The farm produced an assortment of vegetables including potatoes, pumpkins, and beans as well as apples, oranges, pomegranates, figs, peaches, and other fruits. One entry in a family diary mentions that Kell purchased 450 pumpkins from Spooner Forbes to distribute. Another entry says that Shaifer and Forbes took twenty-eight bushels of peaches to Grand Gulf for sale.

3.1. Amanda Guice Shaifer, 1843–1930, whom Kell Shaifer married at the end of the Civil War. She and her friends made the earliest extant quilts in this collection.

3.2. "All Hands Around," maker unknown, in Amanda Guice Shaifer's collection, c. 1865. Of all cotton materials, the quilt is hand-pieced with some machine work and hand-quilted in an overall design ("Baptist Fan") at four to five stitches per inch. It is 85 inches square. Photo courtesy of Mississippi Department of Archives and History.

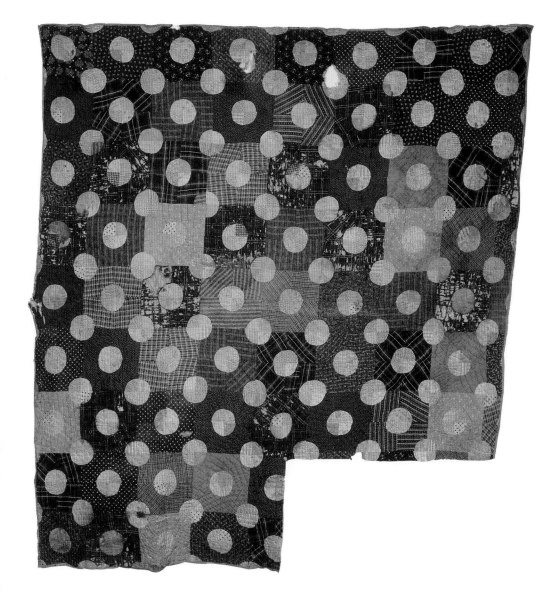

3.3. "Stove Eye" or "Baseball," also known as "Circle," maker unknown, in Amanda Guice Shaifer's collection, c. 1865. Of all cotton materials, the quilt is hand-pieced with some machine work and hand-quilted in an allover design at three stitches per inch. It is 75 inches wide by 82 inches long. No one knows why the corner of the quilt has been crudely cut away, but it was done before Amanda Shaifer's death in 1930. Photo courtesy of Mississippi Department of Archives and History.

As Kell began anew the rhythm of planting and harvesting, Amanda turned her attention to fixing up the house at Holly Hill, returning it to the inviting home it had been before the war.

Amanda Guice Shaifer was a skilled quilter. It is not clear exactly when she started quilting—she was born in 1843 and could have begun sewing as a child of six or so. At least six of her beautifully made quilts remain in the family, along with two that were among her possessions but appear to have been made by someone else. They do not quite match the quality of work known for certain to be from Amanda's hand. Perhaps these two quilts ("All Hands Around" and "Stove Eye") were gifts from friends and neighbors as she set up housekeeping at Holly Hill (to replace those destroyed during the occupation), or maybe they were in Amanda's trousseau, brought from her childhood home.

A review of Amanda's quilts shows her to be very fond of patchwork. Of the seven quilts attributed to her, only one, a pomegranate design, is of appliqué. Three of the quilts—"Pinwheel," "Ocean Waves," and "Corn and Beans"—are made with hundreds of tiny half-square triangles. The "Nine Patch" she made—one of her early quilts—contains sixty-three pieced blocks made of 567 tiny squares (and this was before the concept of speed-piecing was developed!). Her "Log Cabin" is carefully planned and the "logs" are precisely cut. Her color scheme is distinctive in that the center square of each block, said to represent the hearth of the home, is yellow, rather than the traditional red. It is also interesting that she chose pink for the logs on the light side of the square to contrast with the crimson in the same position on the dark side. All five of these patchwork quilts display a

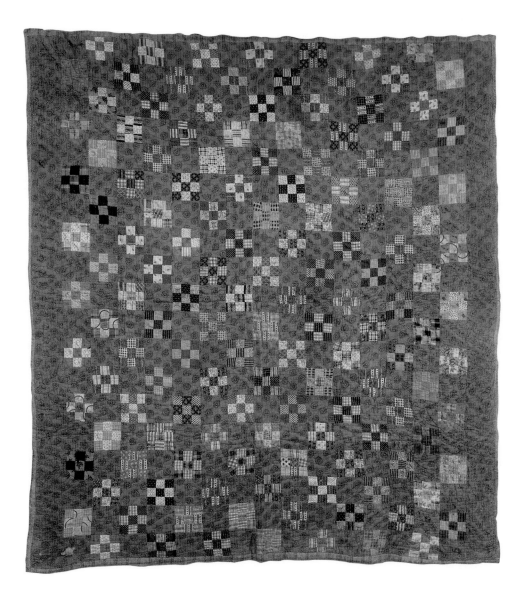

3.4. "Nine Patch," made by Amanda Guice Shaifer, 1865–1870. Of all cotton materials, the quilt is hand-pieced with some machine work and has utilitarian hand-quilting at three stitches per inch. It is 73 inches wide by 78 inches long. Photo courtesy of Mississippi Department of Archives and History.

3.5. "Log Cabin/Straight Furrows," made by Amanda Guice Shaifer, 1875–1890. Of all cotton materials, the quilt is hand-pieced with some machine work and hand-quilted by the piece at six stitches per inch. It is 75 inches wide by 79 inches long. Photo courtesy of Mississippi Department of Archives and History.

3.6. "Corn and Beans," made by Amanda Guice Shaifer, 1880–1900. Of all cotton materials, the quilt is hand-pieced and quilted in an overall fan pattern at four stitches per inch. It is 81 inches wide by 82 inches long. The name of this quilt is reflective of the crops Kell Shaifer farmed, which provided income for the family. Fortunately, neither he nor his father had been in cotton, so he was able to resume the family business after the Civil War. Photo courtesy of Mississippi Department of Archives and History.

3.7. "Pinwheel," made by Amanda Guice Shaifer, 1890–1900. Of all cotton materials, the quilt is hand-pieced with some machine work and hand-quilted by the piece and in a cross-hatch design. It is 80.5 inches wide by 83 inches long. Photo courtesy of Mississippi Department of Archives and History.

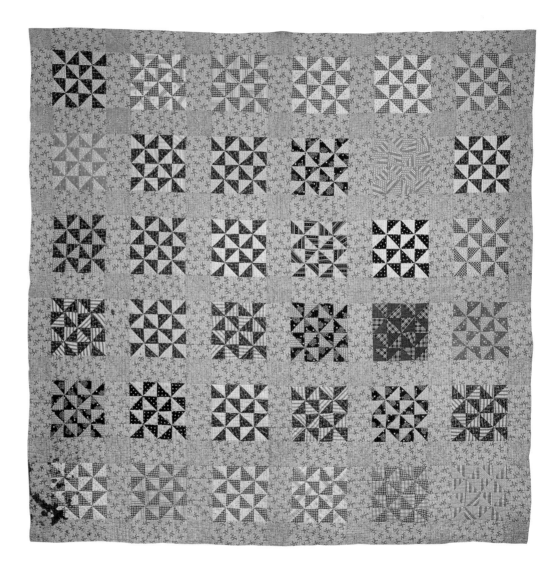

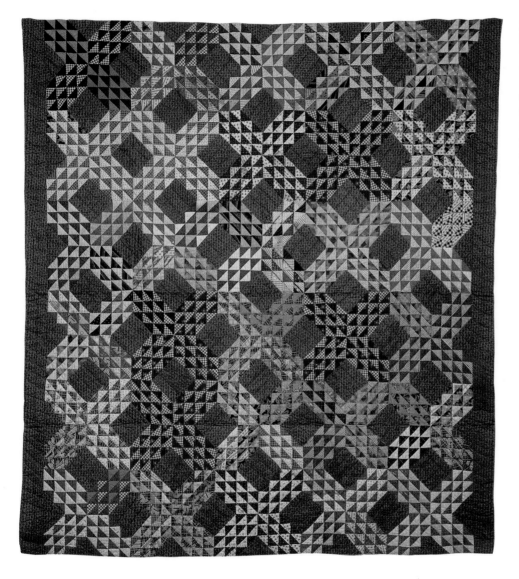

3.8. "Ocean Waves," made by Amanda Guice Shaifer, 1890–1900. Of all cotton materials, the quilt is hand-pieced with some machine work and hand-quilted by the piece at five stitches per inch. It is 71 inches wide by 75 inches long. Photo courtesy of Mississippi Department of Archives and History.

strong, confident sense of color and a sure eye for the placement of the "odd" blocks, so that the rhythm of the design remains in harmony.

The pomegranate appliqué quilt is very traditional in its choice of motif and color scheme. Amanda made it "by the book," without employing her own unique sense of color. Her pomegranate is worked in the red, white, and green color scheme typical of that particular design and the one that many women called upon to execute the quilt they consider the apex of their production. It is something of a puzzle that Amanda made only this one appliquéd quilt; perhaps she was influenced by her quilting friends to give the technique at least one try, but then decided she preferred the technique of piecing.

Evidence that the women of Port Gibson got together to work on quilt projects is presented on the pages of a diary kept by Spooner Forbes, a neighbor (who was an outstanding citizen, a friend of the Shaifers, and one of the appraisers of Elizabeth Humphreys Shaifer's estate). On October 29, 1872, Mr. Forbes recorded, "Wheeless girls here helping Ida with her quilt."[1]

He was referring to Mary Jane Wheeless, who was about eight years younger than Amanda Guice Shaifer and would have been twenty-one years of age at the time of the Forbes's quilting party, and her sister, Elizabeth, born in 1866, who would have been only six at the time. That does not mean that Elizabeth was too young to quilt; it was not at all unusual for young girls and, sometimes, young boys to be piecing simple patchwork by the age of six. Mary Jane and her other sisters, Martha and Sally, had likely begun at that age themselves, because they were known to be fine quilters.

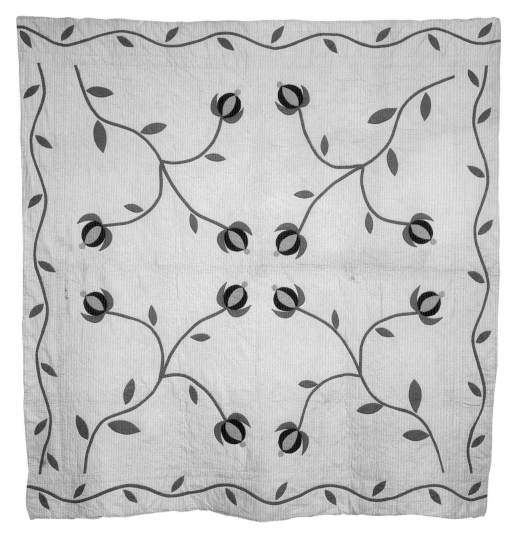

3.9. "Pomegranate," also called "Love Apple" or "Temperance Ball," made by Amanda Guice Shaifer, 1870–1885. Of all cotton materials, the quilt is hand-appliquéd with blind stitch and hand-quilted by the piece and with leafy patterns at five stitches per inch. It is 81 inches wide by 80 inches long. Pomegranates were one of the fruits cultivated by Kell and Amanda Shaifer. Photo courtesy of Mississippi Department of Archives and History.

3.10. Mary Jane Wheeless, 1851–1878, was singled out in Spooner Forbes's diary of 1872 as a quilter of exceptional merit.

On January 22, 1873, Mr. Forbes wrote, "Mrs. Shaifer and the Andrews and Wheeless girls here quilting. Hard rain during the day."[2] This verifies that Amanda and Mary Jane not only knew each other, but also quilted together; indeed, Amanda would become Elizabeth Wheeless's mother-in-law in 1888 when her only son, Percy Leon Shaifer, took Elizabeth as his bride. Meantime, the Wheeless, Forbes, Andrews, and Shaifer girls and women probably gathered frequently to share their hobby. They were all quite skilled, but when Spooner Forbes remarked about the particularly outstanding work of one of the Wheeless girls, it is understood that he was referring to Mary Jane. Sadly, her life was cut short in the yellow fever epidemic of 1878, when she died on August 24 at the age of twenty-seven.

The life that Kell and Amanda built together seems to have been one of happiness and contentment and is certainly an example of industry, compassion, caring, and reconciliation with the Federal forces that fought at Port Gibson. The association with the Union veterans, which became a lifelong allegiance, began as a simple request. One day in the late 1860s, the postmaster at Port Gibson received a letter from an Indiana man, William Duffner, who was interested in establishing contact with someone who had a thorough knowledge of the battlefield upon which he had fought during the Battle of Port Gibson. The postmaster passed the request to Kell, since Holly Hill was the site of the first skirmish of the battle.

Kell enthusiastically took up corresponding with Mr. Duffner and eventually began exchanging letters with Federal soldiers from Ohio and Iowa as well as Indiana.

3.11. "Churn Dash," made by Mary Jane Wheeless, c. 1872. Of all cotton materials, the quilt is hand-pieced and quilted in an all-over shell ("Baptist Fan") pattern at five to six stitches per inch. It is 86.5 inches wide by 87 inches long. Photo courtesy of Mississippi Department of Archives and History.

CHAPTER FOUR

Unique New Friendships

Through his voluminous exchange of letters with the Northern veterans of the Battle of Port Gibson, Kell Shaifer cemented new friendships into place. Inevitably, the swapping of visits and gifts began. The "Boys in Blue" would come down to stay with Amanda and Kell and walk the roads and ridges of the battlefield, returning to the sites where they had seen action. In turn, Kell and Amanda were invited "up there," where they were treated like royalty. Kell was even invited to speak at meetings of Union veterans!

Kell undoubtedly was aware of the questions his friends in Port Gibson must have had about the deep affection he had developed for these men, so recently the hated enemy. The bitterness of Reconstruction and its subsequent overthrow did nothing to create a climate of forgiveness and reconciliation. Kell's remarkably "lovable and genial character" must have been augmented by a keen awareness of time and place, as well as a great deal of soul-searching, as indicated by this passage from one of his letters:

> I have been among the Northern people wearing my Cross of Honor and other Confederate badges and . . . hospitably entertained. . . . Some of my best friends, who were in battle against me, have passed . . . and every Deco-

ration Day I send flowers to decorate their graves. But my heart is . . . true to the Confederacy. . . . Right or wrong, I am a Confederate and I will die one. Because Earl allowed his men to take the featherbed from under my 70-year-old mother, must I forget that Colonel Blackburn dismounted and ministered to me when I was at the point of death on the road to Montrose after the fall of Blakely? [Kell is, of course, describing two different incidents: one was the raid on Holly Hill, where his mother lived with his wife, and the second was his own experience in Alabama, where he was critically wounded at the Battle of Blakely.][1]

The habit of sending flowers from the battlefield to decorate the Union graves on Memorial Day was begun in 1900, after a visit to Mitchell, Indiana. Kell Shaifer maintained this practice until his death. The tradition was, from the beginning, filled with meaning, as evidenced in this letter Kell wrote to Reuben Hart on May 27, 1912:

On account of the overflow on the Mississippi Valley Road, I will start the flowers on their journey Tuesday. I am fearful that they, or some of them, will be wilted when they reach their destination, but not so much so as some of us who took part in that memorable struggle.

Some of the flowers grew on the ridge where the Union line was formed, some where the First Battery was planted in my yard, some where the battle raged the fiercest, and some were presented to me by the ladies of Port Gibson.

Contents of the box: Figs, Oranges, Pomegranates, Magnolias, Cape Jasmine, Rose Buds, Larkspurs, Sweet Olive, Dahlia, Easter Lilies, and Spanish Moss.[2]

Occasionally the boxes shipped to Northern friends included home-made jellies and preserves made by Amanda. The friends reciprocated with gifts of their own, and because they would have known that Amanda was a master quilter, they very likely could have sent her fabrics that would not have been easily available in Port Gibson after the war, such as brocades, tapestries, and velvets. The Northern veterans also made gifts to the Southern veterans, including a sterling silver loving cup, a cup and saucer, a two-volume set of the history of Ohio, and a framed piece of moss from a mill outside of Mitchell (in response to one of Kell's gifts of Spanish moss). One of the most unusual gifts was a chair with a rocker on each of the four legs, an arrangement which produced a bit of a gliding motion. The four-rocker chair is decorated with a painted map of the entire Vicksburg campaign. (The chair is on loan to the Grand Gulf Military Park Museum, located between Port Gibson and Vicksburg.)

Through the years, Amanda Guice Shaifer continued to quilt. One quilt of Amanda's stands out from all her others, in part because it is of fabrics she had never used before, and also because it is so clearly intended as a memory piece—it measures only 29 inches by 37 inches. (All her other quilts are bed sized.) The design is of "Log Cabin" blocks put together in the "Courthouse Steps" style and is stitched of satins, silk brocades, wool twills, and velvets—fabrics thought by the family to be gifts of the Northern friends. The pièce de résistance of the quilt is a silk ribbon on which is written, "Fifth Reunion, United Confederate Veterans, Houston, Texas, May 22, 1895. Compliments Illinois Central R.R." Kell and Amanda were very active in their support of Confederate veterans' groups and looked

4.1. Commemorative quilt, worked in "Courthouse Steps" blocks, made by Amanda Guice Shaifer, 1895. Of silk and other materials, it includes a commemorative ribbon from the fifth reunion of Confederate veterans in Houston, Texas, on May 22, 1895 (compliments of the Illinois Central Railroad). It has a combination of hand and machine work, some embroidery, with machine quilting on cotton backing only. It is 29 inches wide by 37 inches long. Photo courtesy of Mississippi Department of Archives and History.

4.2. A reunion of Federal veterans from Mitchell, Indiana, at Holly Hill in 1901. Amanda stands at the *left*, the only woman in the photograph, with Kell, in a full white beard and light-colored trousers, *beside* her. The Victorian trim across the front porch was probably a modernization of Amanda's, added when she set up housekeeping there after the Battle of Port Gibson.

forward to visiting as many reunions as possible. No doubt they collected the ribbon at one such occasion.

Kell and Amanda hosted a reunion of Civil War veterans at Holly Hill in 1901, but not for Confederates. It was for the Federal veterans of Mitchell, Indiana, and was led, no doubt, by William Duffner, Kell's original correspondent. Kell's memorial to his friend in Duffner's hometown newspaper explains in part the reason for the strong affection between the old soldiers.

[M]y heart went out to him, and I have ever been proud to call him friend. When asked why he never joined the G.A.R. [Grand Army of the Republic, a Union veteran's organization], he answered that, while he was a true Union soldier, when the Confederates laid down their arms, he laid down his, and he never more wanted to say or do anything to grate on the

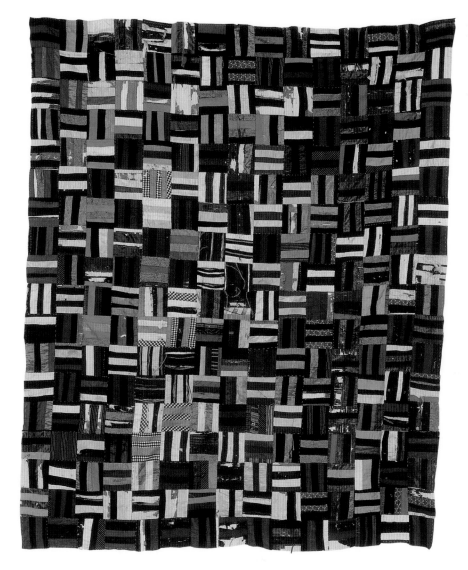

4.3. "String Square" quilt top, made by Amanda Guice Shaifer, 1890–1900. Of silk and other materials, it is hand-pieced. It is 60 inches wide by 73.5 inches long.

feelings of a brave Confederate. A noble sentiment and one that ought to find lodgment in the breast of every man.

He was the first to my knowledge to stretch out his hand across the chasm (not formed by war, but by politicians after the war) and clasp that of a Confederate. Many have since offered me the right hand of fellowship, but he was the original. He seldom ever wrote a letter that he did not send greetings to my Confederate comrades with an invitation to visit him in his home.[3]

An unfinished quilt from this time shows evidence of being from the needle of Amanda Shaifer, made around the same time as the smaller piece containing the ribbon. Pieced in a "String Square" design of four-inch squares, it contains many of the same fabrics that appear in the small commemorative piece. Many of the fabrics have shattered, and the quilt top is very fragile—it invites speculation that it would have survived in better shape if it had been finished in the same manner as the smaller piece. The richness of the fabrics somewhat distracts the eye from the simplicity of the pattern, a design that was originally concocted so that the tiniest snippets of fabric might be utilized in a pieced quilt. Close examination reveals that the strips of the blocks are of uneven widths, and occasionally a shred not much wider than a string has been used to gain the last bit of width required for a four-inch square. Also, just when the viewer becomes convinced that Amanda put exactly five stripes of color in each block, we find a square made of three or four stripes. It really is a string quilt!

The existence of the "String Square" quilt top reinforces a truth to be observed about Amanda Guice Shaifer's quilting: if she tried a style of quilt making once, she experimented with it again and again—in this instance, she played with rectangles, as she had in the little "Courthouse Steps" piece. The exception to this truth was appliqué, and Amanda appears to have made up her mind after one effort that it was not for her, although she was as expert with it as with the other techniques she mastered.

By the 1890s, Kell and Amanda's family consisted of one married son, Benjamin Humphreys Shaifer, who had already given them three granddaughters, and Percy Leon Shaifer, who had, on March 21, 1888, married Elizabeth Wheeless, the young woman who had accompanied her sister to quilt with Percy's mother. (The third son, A. K. Shaifer III, had died of yellow fever at age nineteen. Two other boys Kell had with his first wife died in infancy.)

Kell continued to farm at Holly Hill. In a letter reprinted in the *Port Gibson Reveille* on May 9, 1907, written by Dr. Scott of Fontanello, Iowa, in which he describes a visit to Holly Hill and praises Kell's hospitality, the following comment appears: "His [Kell's] farm consists of 500 acres of red soil which requires much fertilizer and intense farming to make it productive and which he considers almost worthless because of the impossibility of getting help."

A great-grandson of Kell's, Girault McArthur Jones, remembers his great-grandfather well:

4.4. Kell and Amanda Shaifer, sitting in a double rocker in 1919, two years before his death on May 30, 1921. He maintained his correspondence with his Northern friends to the end of his life.

He was a short man, a bit plump in his old age, and with a look very much like Jiggs of the comic strip. Crippled by a back injury, he used crutches in his last years. He sat in his porch swing for hours talking about "the War." He had been held as a prisoner of war on an island off the Mississippi Gulf Coast. I can still hear the very distinct way in which he cleared his throat to announce he had something to say.

. . . Aunt Amanda [father and son had married sisters] was a strikingly handsome woman, taller than her husband, a strong face and a head of snow-white hair, and most memorable of all, a truly remarkable voice. The quiet resonance of a deep but entirely feminine voice brought serenity into any situation. . . . Aunt Amanda was almost regal in her composure. I can see her on that porch in a small circle of people busily peeling figs for preserving. The quiet melody of her speech would lull us until Grandpa Kell suddenly cleared his throat to tell once again some memory of "the War."[4]

Kell departed this life on May 30, 1921, which was, fittingly, a Memorial Day. Amanda continued a vigorous life almost completely to its end on February 22, 1930. She taught and stitched with the succeeding generation of quilters.

CHAPTER FIVE

Mother and Daughter: "Lizzie" and "Dear Laura"

Percy Leon Shaifer and his wife, Elizabeth Wheeless ("Lizzie"), were the first of the Shaifers to make their primary residence in town, rather than on the farm. Percy, after attending Chamberlain-Hunt Academy in Port Gibson, had gone to the College of Emory and Henry, outside Abingdon, Virginia, where he majored in business. Although he had originally planned to start a business of his own when he finished school, he soon became affiliated with the Port Gibson Oil Works.

Known locally as the Oil Mill because its main product was cottonseed oil, the Port Gibson Oil Works was in the business of crushing cottonseed to produce not only oil (which is used in goods such as lard for human consumption), but such byproducts as stuffing for mattresses, in the form of cotton lint, as well as livestock feed, which utilizes cottonseed hulls and cottonseed meal.[1] The fact that this mill was a primary component of Port Gibson's economic life demonstrates that the surrounding area had rebounded after the war and that cotton had again become a primary product of the region.

5.1. Lizzie Wheeless (1866–1953) as a young woman.

5.2. Young Percy Leon Shaifer (1866–1956) as a student at Emory and Henry.

5.3. The Port Gibson home of Percy Leon Shaifer, Kell's son, who married Elizabeth "Lizzie" Wheeless. They lived there from 1904 until the early 1930s. Their three sons were named Edgar D. Shaifer, Abram Keller Shaifer, and Sanfrid Blomquist Shaifer. The daughters were Elizabeth Estelle and Laura Percy. Sanfrid Blomquist Shaifer married Dorothy Davidson, and they are the parents of the current generation of Port Gibson Shaifers.

The early quilts Lizzie made are very similar to those of her mother-in-law, Amanda Guice Shaifer, who was her close neighbor and friend before she became her mother-in-law. Amanda's quilts are notable for their deep, rich color schemes that make sparing use of white. The first of Lizzie's quilts are scrap quilts, the colors of which are masterfully blended in obvious imitation of Amanda's style. Lizzie's "Nine-Patch" almost echoes Amanda's "Ocean Waves." Lizzie's "This or That" not only uses color in a way much akin to Amanda's "Pinwheel," but also makes use of the half-square triangle that so fascinated Amanda.

There are two additional quilts from around 1885, when Lizzie was nineteen years old and not yet married. These are different from the other quilts she was making then, and they give a hint as to the direction her use of color was heading. These two quilts are an "Album Cross" and a "Dove at the Window" quilt top. The "Album Cross" is made with a potpourri of scraps (some of the same fabrics that appear in the "Stove Eye" quilt that belonged to Amanda and is about thirty years older), but it is sashed and bordered in white. The "Dove at the Window" quilt top, although made of nothing but prints, utilizes a very neutral, airy print for the background, one that gives the impression of white. With these two quilts, Lizzie was moving toward a style of her own, one that would make use of white backgrounds almost exclusively.

Lizzie and Percy began their married life out in the country, about halfway between Holly Hill and the Wheeless home. Children soon began arriving. The first child, Edgar, was born ten months after the wedding day, on January 26, 1889; Laura arrived three years almost to the day after her brother, on January 19, 1892; then came Elizabeth Estelle, on February 1,

5.4. "Nine-Patch," made by Elizabeth "Lizzie" Wheeless Shaifer, c. 1885. Of all cotton materials, the quilt is hand-pieced with some machine work and hand-quilted in an all-over design of shells ("Baptist Fan") at five stitches per inch. It is 80 inches square. Photo courtesy of Mississippi Department of Archives and History.

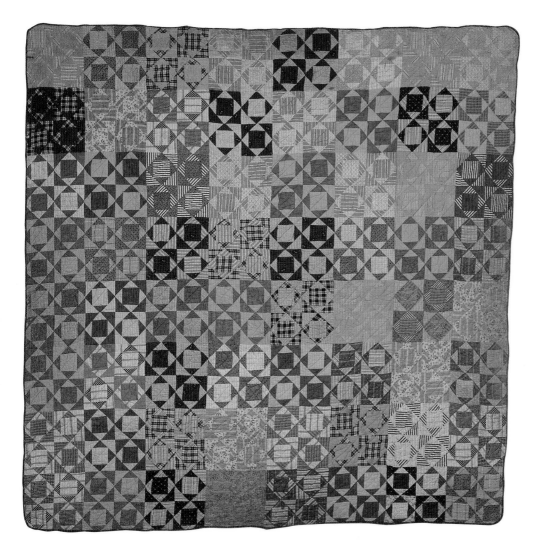

5.5. "This or That," made by Elizabeth Wheeless Shaifer, c. 1885. Of all cotton materials, the quilt is hand-pieced with some machine work and machine-quilted in an all-over design of diagonal lines. It is 78 inches square. Photo courtesy of Mississippi Department of Archives and History.

5.6. "Dove at the Window," quilt top made by Elizabeth "Lizzie" Wheeless Shaifer, c. 1885. Of cotton ("double" or "cinnamon" pinks, white ground with black motif shirting prints, indigo prints), it is 80 inches wide by 102 inches long.

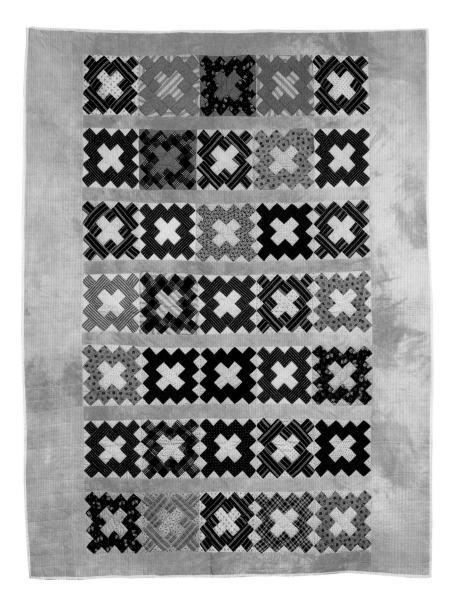

5.7. "Album Cross," made by Elizabeth "Lizzie" Wheeless Shaifer, c. 1885. Of cotton materials for top and backing and with a wool sheet for a batting, the quilt is hand-pieced and quilted at five stitches per inch. It is 70.5 inches wide by 91 inches long. Photo courtesy of Mississippi Department of Archives and History.

5.8 Laura Percy Shaifer, "Dear Laura," 1892–1982, at her graduation from Port Gibson High School in 1911.

1897; Abram Keller, on September 13, 1898; and Sanfrid Blomquist, on September 5, 1902. This last birth occurred the same year that Percy and Lizzie moved into town. Two years later they were settled into a brand-new house in which they reared their five children and lived for the next thirty years.

Laura became known to the family as "Dear Laura" in her early adulthood. A four-year-old niece (Libby Shaifer Hollingsworth) asked her Aunt Ada how to begin a thank-you note. Aunt Ada replied by using an example the niece could understand, "Dear Laura." The niece misinterpreted Aunt Ada's instructions regarding salutations, believing instead that she had finally learned her Aunt Laura's real name. The pet name was such an excellent match for Laura's temperament that it stayed with her from that day forward.

Perhaps because Lizzie was busy with the children and taking care of aging parents, there are no quilts clearly attributable to her during most of the first two decades of the twentieth century. She continued to do other types of needlework, but maybe she put quilting aside because of the space required to put together and quilt a whole quilt. (Coincidentally, this was the time when national interest in quilting was at its lowest ebb in years, probably as a result of a general boredom with the all-pervasive crazy quilt fad that had held the quilting world enraptured for more than twenty years. See *Mississippi Quilts* for more information.[2])

After a hiatus of fifteen years or more, Lizzie took up her needle to quilt again when her youngest child was up and out of the house. By this time Dear Laura was an accomplished needlewoman, and she joined her mother and grandmother in talking about quilts, making quilts, and giv-

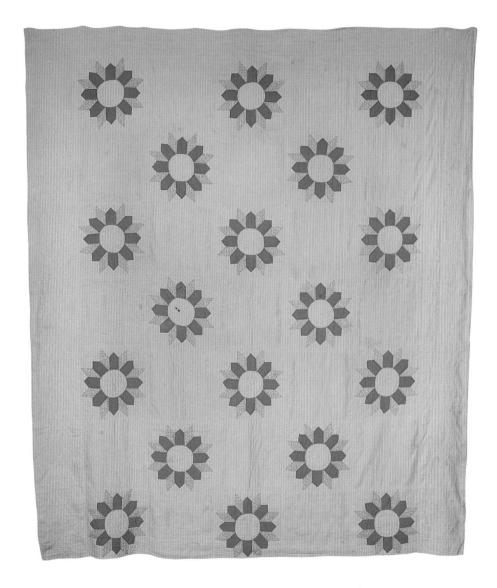

5.9. "The Gardener's Prize," made by Elizabeth "Lizzie" Wheeless Shaifer, 1920s. Of all cotton materials, the quilt has a combination of hand-piecing and appliqué with a blind stitch; it is hand-quilted by the piece and with a floral design in setting blocks. It is 88 inches wide by 106 inches long.

5.10. "Drunkard's Path" variation, made by Elizabeth "Lizzie" Wheeless Shaifer, 1920s. Of all cotton materials, the quilt has a combination of hand and machine work and is hand-quilted at seven stitches per inch. It is 80 inches wide by 81.5 inches long.

5.11. "Pinwheel" with "Saw-tooth" border, made by Elizabeth "Lizzie" Wheeless Shaifer, 1920s. Of all cotton materials, the quilt has a combination of hand and machine work.

5.12. Beginning in the first decade of the twentieth century, the Shaifer women began to work with commercial patterns and quilt kits. Photo courtesy of Mississippi Department of Archives and History.

ing quilts away. Although each woman produced her own quilts, Amanda, Lizzie, and Dear Laura often worked together in the years between 1910 and 1930, with Dear Laura being warmly welcomed into the quilting companionship that Lizzie and Amanda had shared for years. Lizzie and Dear Laura continued to work together after Amanda's death in 1930.

When Lizzie resumed quilting, she first stitched the distinctively light and open patchwork pieces of the 1920s: "A Gardener's Prize" and a variation of "Rob Peter to Pay Paul," set into the "Drunkard's Path" design, as well as a "Pinwheel" with a "Sawtooth" border. Although the finished quilts are quite different from one another, they are similar in that they are all made by piecing, rather than appliqué, and they all make use of solid fabrics in medium tones. They do not appear to be made from remnants from the scrap bag; it seems very possible that Lizzie not only purchased fabric specifically for the quilts, but may have also been persuaded to buy the newest thing on the market for those who loved to quilt—commercially printed quilt patterns.

Since Port Gibson is located almost exactly halfway between Vicksburg and Natchez—two of the five largest towns in the state by 1910—it was likely that the Shaifer women easily found what they wanted when they shopped for fabrics and quilting supplies. If a particular pattern was not locally available, it could easily be ordered through any number of magazines, and when that pattern arrived in the mail, it would be accompanied by a catalog of other designs that were available.

As counter-intuitive as it seems that a person would purchase a pattern for a simple patchwork design like "Pinwheel," the first patterns to be available to quilters were, for the most part, based on traditional designs from the nineteenth century, a result of a national interest in the American past that came about after World War I.[3] Whereas in the nineteenth century quilt patterns were exchanged person to person, all patterns were now available to everyone, and an early twentieth-century quilter could be exposed, through one catalog, to more quilt designs than a nineteenth-century quilter would have seen in a lifetime. So, although the "Pinwheel" quilt that Lizzie made is a variation of a design that Amanda made forty-plus years earlier (see fig. 3.7), it seemed "modern" because it had been manufactured as a commercial pattern.

5.13. Percy Leon Shaifer and Elizabeth "Lizzie" Wheeless in the 1940s.

In 1930, Percy and Lizzie, as a result of an unexpected financial windfall, were able to build a new house on Church Street in Port Gibson; it remains the Shaifer home today. The house is in the Italianate style, and it provided a completely different lifestyle for the now-retired couple. Not only was the architecture completely different from the Victorian home they had lived in before, but the new house was also replete with all the conveniences that 1930s technology could offer. Percy and Lizzie moved in with two daughters, one of whom, Estelle, soon married and moved to her own home. Dear Laura never married; instead, she spent the rest of her life contentedly taking care of her parents and the house.

A trove of quilt ephemera was stored in a box underneath one of the beds in the Shaifer home. Among hand-drawn quilting designs, quilting

5.14. "Double Nine Patch" or "The 'H' Block," made by Elizabeth "Lizzie" Wheeless Shaifer, 1920–1930. Of all cotton materials, the quilt is hand-pieced and quilted. It is 77 inches wide by 80 inches long.

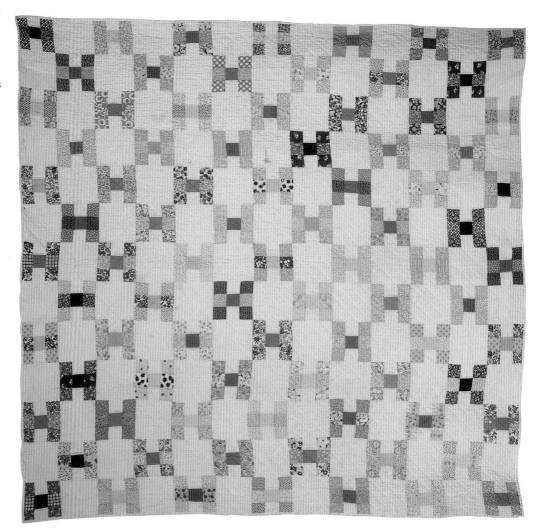

hoops, embroidery scissors, designs for pillowcase embroidery, and other miscellany were nine commercial quilt patterns from well-known manufacturers of the 1920s and 1930s. Three are from Ann Orr, who was needlecraft editor of *Good Housekeeping* magazine from 1919 to 1940; she also had a business under her own name that published booklets of quilt patterns, manufactured quilt kits, and produced finished quilts for sale. Three patterns are from Laura Wheeler, a pseudonym used for the author of a syndicated newspaper needlework column still being published, although no longer with an "author;" one is from Nancy Cabot of the *Chicago Tribune,* who published eight hundred quilt patterns over a ten-year period;[4] one is from McCall's pattern company; the ninth, for an iris appliqué, is without its packaging, so its source is unknown.

One of the interesting aspects of this collection of patterns is the breadth and depth of design styles that it covers. The Laura Wheeler patterns are traditional, but complicated, patchwork designs—the pieced "Snowball Wreath" is anything but simple. Ann Orr was noted for designs that look like early computer printouts, with angles instead of curves for flower petals and leaves; that is because Orr drew many of her quilt designs on gridded graph paper, having begun her career by drawing cross-stitch charts.[5] Another of the patterns is for a whole-cloth quilt; a third Ann Orr design is for a beautiful appliquéd iris (not in the "computer-graphic" mode, but more realistic). The range of styles in this selection of commercial quilt patterns suggests that the Shaifer women were attracted to that which was new and interesting, that they sought out challenges, and that they read widely. (The "Drunkard's Path" design that Lizzie used is listed in twelve different sources in a popular quilt pattern identification guide.[6]

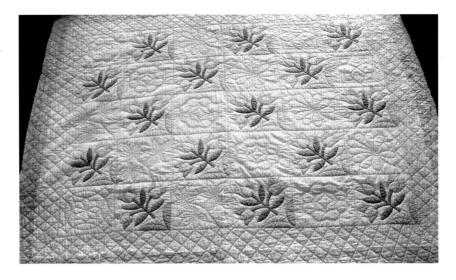

5.15. "Triple Tulips," made by Elizabeth "Lizzie" Wheeless Shaifer, late 1920s. Of all cotton materials, the quilt is hand-appliquéd with blind stitch, has some machine work, and is hand-quilted by the piece and with multiple rows in setting blocks at five stitches per inch. It is 76 inches wide by 85 inches long.

That is not to say that the Shaifer women read all twelve of those sources, but that they could hardly have missed seeing the design, since it was so widely published.)

Lizzie's "Double Nine-Patch," or "'H' Block," made in the late 1920s or early 1930s, can be considered a transitional piece; it is done with a familiar technique, but with materials different from her usual choices. A traditional patchwork design, probably from a commercial pattern, the quilt is worked in many different colors (probably from the scrap bag), rather than in the two or three to which Lizzie had restricted herself in previous quilts. Even though it is very colorful, the quilt retains the light and airy feeling of Lizzie's earlier work because of the use of white setting blocks. (The next time Lizzie would turn to the scrap bag for fabrics would be for the "Dresden Plate" she made later in the 1930s.)

Evidence that Lizzie was stretching her range, enlarging her design and skill abilities, may be found in another 1920s quilt. "Triple Tulips" marks a departure from the pieced quilts she had always preferred: it was Lizzie's first appliquéd quilt. Although she had, to the family's knowledge, never made an entire quilt of appliqué, or even experimented with smaller appliqué pieces, "Triple Tulips" is perfectly stitched. (There is a strong possibility that Dear Laura, who was quite fond of appliqué, assisted in the making of this quilt, but Lizzie did the majority of the work.) Although the design could have come from a commercial pattern, it is more likely that the quilt is from an early kit; this conclusion is indicated by the subtle gradation of the pink-rose color scheme. Unless the local Michael Ellis Department Store carried an unusually large stock of fabric, a wide range of shades in solid colors would not have been available. Usually there would be one or two offerings of solids in a particular color family, and the remainder of the fabric stock would be prints. One clue to identifying a kit quilt is a sophisticated color scheme that uses closely related shades and tints of one particular color to make up a flower or some other design element.

Once she began working with appliqué, Lizzie apparently enjoyed it. Her next quilt was a sprightly design of shamrocks, four to a block in forty-two blocks—168 shamrocks are surely a testament to an affinity for appliqué! Additionally, there are two exquisitely appliquéd central medallion floral quilts, "Old-Fashioned Spray" and "Floral Basket," both made from kits.

The presence of a package of "Grandmother Clark's Blue Stamping Powder" in the box of quilting supplies suggests that Lizzie and Amanda

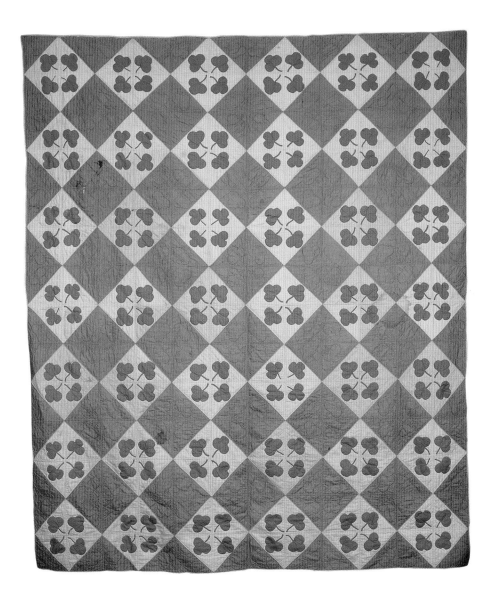

5.16. "Shamrock," made by Elizabeth "Lizzie" Wheeless Shaifer, 1930s. Of all cotton materials, the quilt is hand-pieced and appliquéd with a blind stitch and hand-quilted at six stitches per inch. It is 90 inches wide by 106 inches long. Photo courtesy of Mississippi Department of Archives and History.

5.17. "Old-Fashioned Spray" kit quilt, made by Elizabeth "Lizzie" Wheeless Shaifer, 1930s. Of all cotton materials, the quilt is hand-appliquéd with some machine work and hand-quilted at seven stitches per inch. It is 75 inches wide by 95 inches long. Photo courtesy of Mississippi Department of Archives and History.

5.18. "Floral Basket" kit quilt, made by Elizabeth "Lizzie" Wheeless Shaifer, 1930s. Of all cotton materials for top and backing, with a wool batting, the quilt is hand-appliquéd with blind stitch. It is 74.5 inches wide by 92 inches long. Photo courtesy of Mississippi Department of Archives and History.

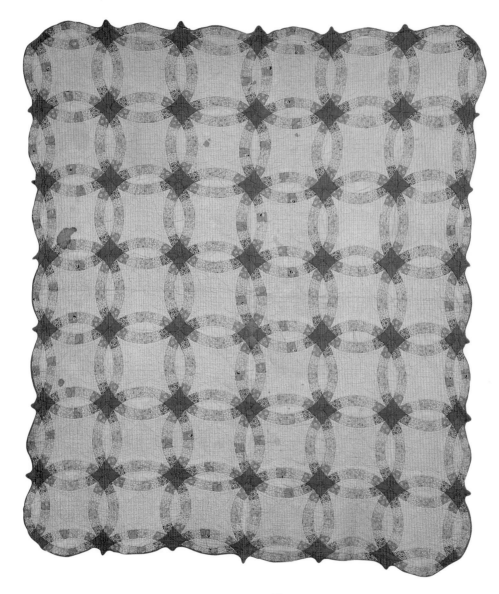

5.19. "Double Wedding Ring," made by Elizabeth "Lizzie" Wheeless Shaifer, 1930s. Of cotton material for top and backing, with a wool batting, the quilt is hand-pieced and quilted at six stitches per inch. It is 66 inches wide by 76.5 inches long. Photo courtesy of Mississippi Department of Archives and History.

5.20. "Dresden Plate," in the "Dessert Plate" variation, made by Elizabeth "Lizzie" Wheeless Shaifer, 1930s. Of all cotton materials for top and backing, with a wool batting, the quilt has a combination of hand-piecing and appliqué with buttonhole or blanket stitch and is hand-quilted by the piece at eight stitches per inch. It is 80 inches wide by 95.75 inches long. Photo courtesy of Mississippi Department of Archives and History.

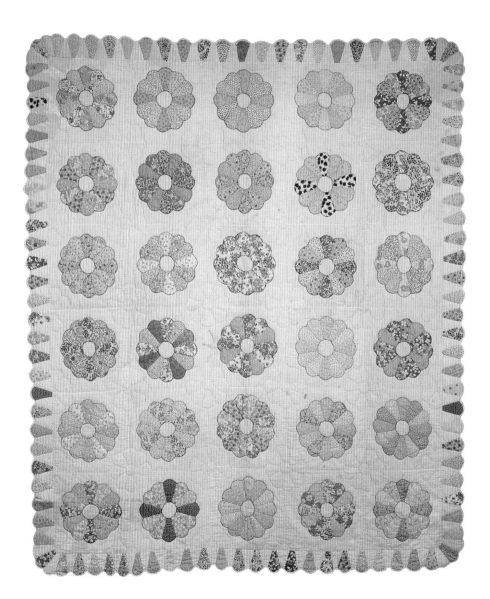

5.21. "Three Tulips," made by Laura Percy Shaifer, 1930s. The quilt is hand-appliquéd with a blind stitch, has some machine work, and is quilted by the piece and in a cross-hatch design at five stitches per inch. It is 69 inches wide by 89.5 inches long. Photo courtesy of Mississippi Department of Archives and History.

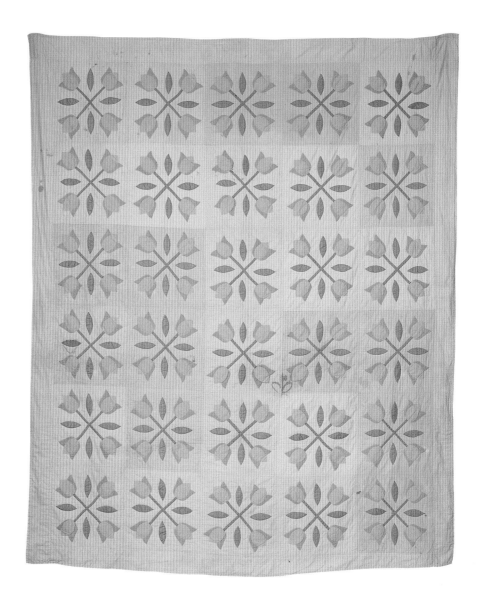

5.22. "Crossed Tulips," made by Laura Percy Shaifer, 1940. Of all cotton materials, the quilt is hand-appliquéd with a blind stitch and hand-quilted by the piece at five stitches per inch. It is 81.5 inches wide by 99.25 inches long.

5.23. "Meadow Lily," made by Elizabeth "Lizzie" Wheeless Shaifer (with possible help from Laura Percy Shaifer), 1944. Of all cotton materials, the quilt has a combination of hand-piecing and appliqué with a buttonhole or blanket stitch and is hand-quilted by the piece at five to six stitches per inch. It is 76.5 inches wide by 86 inches long. Photo courtesy of Mississippi Department of Archives and History.

5.24. "Basketweave," made by Laura Percy Shaifer, 1935–1940. Of all cotton materials, the quilt is hand-pieced with some machine work and hand-quilted by the piece with "Baptist Fan" design in border. It is 84 inches square.

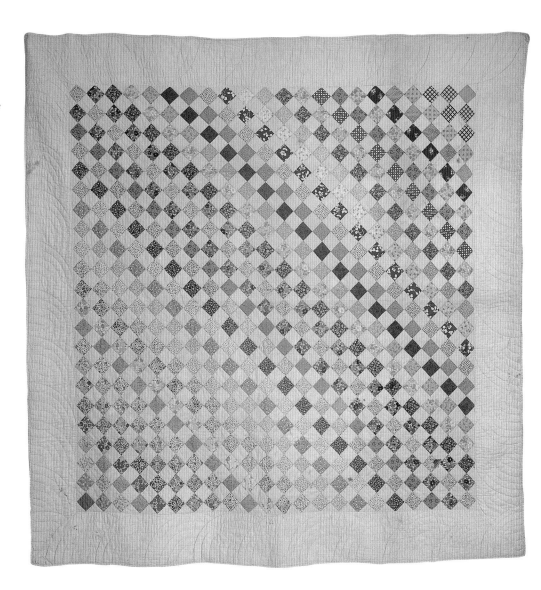

5.25. "Double Irish Chain," made by Laura Percy Shaifer and Elizabeth Wheeless Shaifer, 1934. Of all cotton materials, the quilt is hand-pieced with some machine work and hand-quilted in an all-over square grid at four to five stitches per inch. It is 68 inches wide by 74 inches long.

5.26. "Grandmother's Flower Garden," made by Laura Percy Shaifer, 1940s. Of all cotton materials, the quilt is hand-pieced and quilted. It is 60 inches wide by 69 inches long. Photo courtesy of Mississippi Department of Archives and History.

5.27. "Whirling Star," made by Laura Percy Shaifer, 1935–1940. Of all cotton materials (some polished cotton), the quilt is hand-pieced and quilted by the piece. It is 74.5 inches wide by 85 inches long. Photo courtesy of Mississippi Department of Archives and History.

5.28. Letter from Ben Shaifer Jones, great grandson of "Kell" Shaifer, to his mother Elizabeth "Money" Shaifer, used to draw a "Butterfly" pattern, dated 1932. When not ordering kits or commercial patterns, Dear Laura and Lizzie resorted to creating their own.

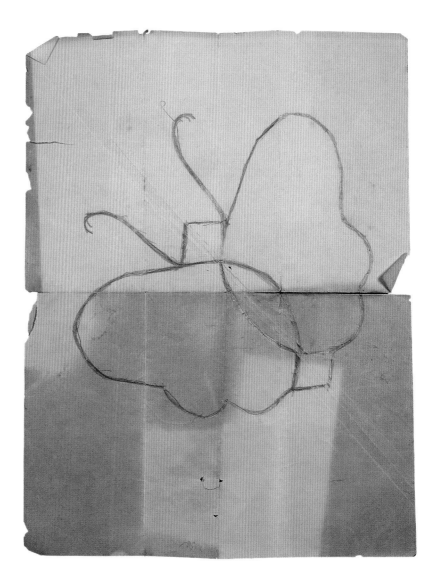

and Dear Laura began their experimentation with quilt kits on some of the first ones available. The very early quilt kits were fairly labor-intensive and did not save the quilter much time. The kit included a line drawing on a large sheet of paper that had to be perforated with a tracing wheel. Then the pattern was laid on top of the fabric that would serve as the background, and stamping powder was rubbed through the tiny holes to transfer the design onto the fabric. Blue was used for light-colored backgrounds, and yellow for dark. It was not until iron-on transfers and pre-stamped fabrics were developed that quilt kits gained a noticeable slice of the quilt retail business. However, the fact that the three Shaifer women were willing to go through the hassle of those early kits underlines their willingness to try new and unproven innovations in quilting.

It is apparent from her work that Lizzie became quite fond of appliqué, and when she returned to her first love, piecing, she used the technique differently than she ever had before, by making two segmented circle designs—"Double Wedding Ring" and "Dresden Plate." The second quilt utilized both techniques in its construction: piecing to make the segmented "plates" and appliqué to stitch them to the background. Also on this quilt, Lizzie used a feature she had tried only once before—a pieced border. This one, made of "ice cream cones" (really one segment of the plates), was probably included in the pattern for the "Dresden Plate" quilt.

Dear Laura, twenty-eight years old in 1920, considered commercial quilt patterns merely a fact of life, as they had been around ever since she began quilting, and she regularly made use of them. Because Dear Laura was talented in so many areas—painting, cooking, gardening, rug-hooking—she may not have begun quilting quite as early as had her mother and grand-

5.29. "Butterfly," made by Elizabeth Wheeless Shaifer and Dear Laura Shaifer, c. 1935. Of all cotton materials, the quilt is hand-appliquéd with embroidered blanket stitch in black and hand-quilted at five stitches per inch by the piece with additional motifs of feathered wreaths and crosshatching. It is 72 inches wide by 84 inches long. Photo courtesy of Mississippi Department of Archives and History.

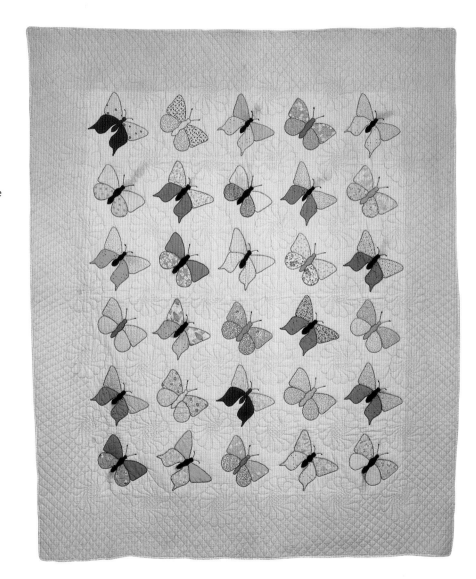

mother. The earliest quilt that she is known to have worked on is the "Triple Tulip" made by her mother in the 1920s. However, she must have made other quilts before then, because this is hardly a beginner's project, and the work is quite good.

One thing is certain: Dear Laura had a passion for tulips! Of the nine quilts on which she either worked or made by herself, four of them are tulip designs. After helping her mother with the first one, the pink one, Dear Laura made two, perhaps three, more tulip quilts, each different from the others. She made one with blue flowers in the 1930s, one in yellow in the 1940s (which she spread on the dining room table to quilt), and a multicolor one in 1944. All are appliqué, with the last one differing from the others in that it is a combination of appliqué and piecework and is made of prints instead of the solid fabrics used for the other three tulip quilts. This third quilt was primarily Lizzie's project; it bears the same characteristics as her "Double Wedding Ring" (fig. 5.19) and "Dresden Plate" (fig. 5.20), but Dear Laura undoubtedly helped her mother with this, her favorite motif.

Dear Laura was also quite happy making patchwork quilts. She made a sweet little one-patch of two-inch squares set on point so that lines of the same fabric run diagonally across the quilt; because the colored squares are interspersed with muslin squares, the effect is of woven ribbons. She made a very nice scrappy "Grandmother's Flower Garden," which today, as a result of unfortunate laundering sometime in its past that has caused the thread to shrink, is so wrinkled as to appear deliberately ruched. The most outstanding of Dear Laura's pieced quilts is a "Whirling Star" made from a Laura Wheeler pattern sold through a syndicate with an address at Old

Chelsea Station, New York. (So many familiar quilt patterns were sold through this post office that they became known simply as OCS patterns.) Dear Laura cleverly arranged her color placement so that a secondary pattern of whirling stars with alternating green and yellow blades dominates the overall quilt.

As Lizzie (known affectionately by the townspeople of Port Gibson as "Aunt Lizzie") grew older, the terrible arthritis of the back that always plagued her grew worse; although she used a cane, she was never able to walk much at all. Her hands, however, were always busy. "Mamma's hands were never still," says her granddaughter, Libby Shaifer Hollingsworth. Lizzie crocheted, tatted, embroidered, and cut and hemmed all the household linens. She made eleven quilts on her own and three more with Dear Laura, but this is likely not the total of Elizabeth Wheeless Shaifer's production. She made quilts as gifts, as evidenced by the one she and Dear Laura made for her grandson upon the occasion of his birth on June 14, 1934 (see fig. 5.25). Although this particular quilt has found its way back home to the Shaifer collection, it is quite possible that Lizzie gave away many quilts that have stayed with the recipients.

CHAPTER SIX

Into the Twenty-First Century: New Talent Joins the Shaifers

The guardian of the entire Shaifer quilt collection these days is Elizabeth Shaifer Hollingsworth, granddaughter of Lizzie Shaifer and niece of Dear Laura. The current Elizabeth, better known as "Libby," has vivid memories of growing up in the company of her kinswomen. Lizzie was sixty-seven years old and Dear Laura was only forty-one when Libby was born, so Libby had twenty years with her grandmother and nearly forty with Dear Laura.

Libby's mother, Dorothy Davidson "Dot" Shaifer, married Lizzie's son, Sanfrid Blomquist (Shag) Shaifer, and they set up housekeeping first in Indianola, then in Leland, Mississippi. Shag had followed his father into the cottonseed oil business, and he and Dot had two children—a daughter, Libby, and a son, Sanfrid Davidson (Sammy) Shaifer. Dot continues to spend part of the year in the Port Gibson home, accompanied by Libby and her husband, Al Hollingsworth, a native of Greenville, Mississippi.

Dot Shaifer is a quilter and has one extremely interesting quilt in her

6.1. Virginia Brown Baker (1860–1911), Dot Shaifer's maternal grandmother, was born at Beauvoir, originally known as Orange Grove, but now famous as the post–Civil War home of Jefferson Davis. Virginia's one quilt contains scraps of clothing worn by the original owners of Beauvoir.

6.2. Joseph Holmes Baker, Dot Shaifer's maternal grandfather, was state senator from Sunflower County, Mississippi, from 1892 to 1894. The blue scarf that Virginia gave him to wear to the legislature appears in her crazy quilt.

own family background. The lineage of this quilt stretches from Mississippi's Gulf Coast to Sunflower County.

Dot Shaifer's maternal grandmother, Virginia Brown, was born on March 2, 1860, at the house now known as Beauvoir in Biloxi; her parents built the house in the early 1850s. It was originally named Orange Grove because of the citrus trees on the property; a nearby town retains the name of Orange Grove today. Mr. Brown died during the Civil War or shortly afterward, and the family was unable to keep the house. The Browns' neighbor, Sarah Ann Dorsey, bought Orange Grove and gave it to Jefferson Davis, the ex-president of the Confederacy, who renamed it Beauvoir ("beautiful view"). Some of the original Brown furnishings, including a large sideboard, remain with the house today.

Upon the sale of Orange Grove, the Browns moved to Indianola. It was not until after Virginia Brown had married Joseph Holmes Baker, a young Indianola lawyer who represented Sunflower County in the state senate from 1892 to 1894, that she decided to put together a quilt, probably the

6.3. "Crazy Quilt," made by Virginia Brown Baker, Indianola, Mississippi, 1895. Of silks, wools, velvets, brocades, the quilt's backing is cotton in a gold color and is brought to the front as a binding. It is 64 inches wide by 75.5 inches long. Photo courtesy of Mississippi Department of Archives and History.

6.4. Dorothy "Dot" Davidson Shaifer (1908–) at about thirty-three years of age.

only one she ever made. It does not appear that she was a devoted quilter—she painted china and did other crafts and was the head of the Women's Christian Temperance Union in her area, so she stayed busy with creative endeavors and was active in the community. She was probably drawn to the idea of making a crazy quilt for the reason so many other non-quilters were attracted to the form: it was a way of keeping a lasting record of special memories.

Virginia Brown Baker chose her materials for the quilt with care. She began with the wedding clothes of her father and mother, plus her mother's "second day" dress. She incorporated her own wedding dress and a blue patterned silk scarf she had given her husband, the new senator, to wear during his term in the state legislature. There are many other fabrics as well, but it is not known if they held particular significance to Virginia. She obviously had been well schooled in the art of embroidery, because the quilt is covered with a great variety of inventive and beautiful stitches.

Virginia Brown Baker's crazy quilt is in relatively good condition, considering the fragility of the fabrics with which it is made. Mrs. Baker's descendents take a great deal of pleasure in the quilt, and it was a center of attention when it was displayed at a great-great-great-granddaughter's wedding reception in the 1990s at Beauvoir.

When Dot Shaifer joined the family as a bride in 1930, she took much creative energy into a family already teeming with it. Among her passions were, and continue to be, gardening, bird-watching, and flower arranging. That is perhaps the reason that her choice of a new quilt to appliqué or cross-stitch was almost always of a floral motif. Or perhaps the spirit of

6.5. "The Iris," a kit quilt from an Ann Orr design of 1935, appliquéd by Dorothy "Dot" Davidson Shaifer and quilted by Elizabeth Wheeless "Lizzie" Shaifer and Laura Percy "Dear Laura" Shaifer, 1935–1936. Of all cotton materials, the quilt is hand-appliquéd with a blind stitch and hand-quilted in various designs at five to six stitches per inch. It is 76.5 inches wide by 87 inches long. Photo courtesy of Mississippi Department of Archives and History.

the Art Nouveau movement, which taught that nature was the ultimate in beauty, influenced her. Thousands of quilts with flower, leaf, or tree themes were made between 1900 and 1950, the result of the influence of Art Nouveau. Many of the designs were literal interpretations, but others were stylized into graceful curves that were especially suited for appliqué. A perfect example of the genre is Dot's "Iris" quilt.

Kits and patterns were, in the 1930s, continuing to fuel the interest in quilting, prolonging a trend that began in the 1920s and, as we have seen, greatly influenced the quilts of Dot's mother-in-law and sisters-in-law. This was a time during which a great deal of new information was being published about the decorative arts, ranging from Japanese to Egyptian, to the styles of Art Nouveau and Art Deco. All these influences found their way into quilt designs, and it was through manufactured kits that a quilter could take advantage of the beautiful new motifs she saw in drapery and upholstery fabric, furniture, china, lamps, and other household accessories.

Many quilt pattern companies and publications hired prominent artists, such as Maxfield Parrish, to do a few designs for them, which added a prestigious luster to quilt patterns, although the artists did not concern themselves with how the designs were to be sewn together![1] The regular designers of quilt patterns and kits, even if they weren't internationally famous, were professional artists, and as such commanded the admiration and patronage of quilters across the country. National magazines and newspapers helped to create a following for certain designers by promoting their work in editorial features; and, in many instances, quilt kits and/or patterns were offered as incentives to subscribe to a particular publication.

It may be difficult for today's quilter to understand the importance of quilt kits and patterns because this is a time in which originality is prized above almost all else, with patterns, and especially kits, being scorned as the province of the rank beginner. However, if one is to understand the mindset of the early twentieth-century quilter, one must accept the enthusiasm she had for commercial patterns and kits. Thomas K. Woodard and Blanche Greenstein, acknowledged experts on quilts of that period, forcefully state this.

Just as many a sewer today would never dream of making a dress without buying a pattern from Butterick or McCall's, quilters in the early twentieth century considered a pattern a natural prerequisite to cutting out a quilt. With this as a guide, they were able to lay out and complete complicated spreads. And they gained access to an abundance of sophisticated designs that otherwise might not have reached their communities.

. . . quilters in the 1920s and 1930s were less concerned with a pattern's uniqueness and were more interested in being able to complete a difficult quilt skillfully.

. . . the pattern [and kit] business thrived because of tremendous demand. When a woman's quilt was displayed at a store or awarded a prize, be it the Grand Prize at a world's fair or an honorable mention in a regional contest, she was usually inundated with letters inquiring about her pattern.[2]

As unbelievable as it might seem by today's standards, quilts that had been made from patterns or kits took the top prizes in many prestigious quilt contests. Three of the five top winners in the 1933 Sears "National

6.6. "Poinsettia," a pattern from Stearns and Foster's Mountain Mist quilt batting, appliquéd by Dot Shaifer, who was assisted in the quilting by Elizabeth "Lizzie" Shaifer and Dear Laura Shaifer, c. 1940. Of all cotton materials, the quilt is hand-appliquéd with a blind stitch and hand-quilted by the piece and with cross-hatching in the background at four stitches per inch.

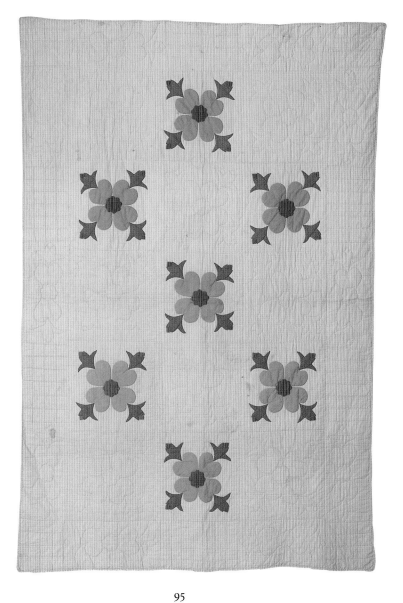

6.7. "Ohio Rose," a pattern from Stearns and Foster's Mountain Mist quilt batting, appliquéd by Dot Shaifer, perhaps professionally quilted, c. 1935. Of all cotton materials, the quilt is hand-appliquéd with a blind stitch and hand-quilted by the piece and with a floral design in setting blocks and borders at seven to eight stitches per inch. It is 64 inches wide by 94 inches long. (It is one of a pair made when twin beds were purchased.)

6.8. "Pink Dogwood," kit quilt appliquéd by Dot Shaifer, 1970s. Of all cotton materials, some polished cotton, it is 74 inches wide by 92 inches long.

6.9. Dear Laura, her brother A. K. (the fourth Abram Keller Shaifer), and Dot and Shag Shaifer with Sam Magruder of the Claiborne County Historical Society. They stand in front of the Shaifer home on Church Street. This is the most recent house built by the Shaifer family in Port Gibson and was constructed in 1930 by Percy and Lizzie Shaifer. It descended to Shag and Dot Shaifer, then to the current generation, Libby and Al Hollingsworth.

6.10. Libby Hollingsworth as a youngster.

Quilt Contest and Century of Progress Exposition" were made from commercial patterns or kits.[3]

Dot Shaifer took full advantage of the many wonderful quilt kits and patterns that were available. She appliquéd, in addition to the fabulous "Iris" quilt, four more floral quilts: a "Poinsettia," a pattern available from a Stearns and Foster quilt batting package wrapper; two in the "Ohio Rose" pattern, another from Stearns and Foster known by many names, one of which is "Colonial Rose"; and a "Pink Dogwood," a kit quilt made spectacular by the use of a very pretty soft green background.

Dear Laura lived with Lizzie and Percy in the Church Street home until their deaths in 1951 and 1952, respectively. She continued to live there alone, welcoming the family whenever they could make it to Port Gibson for a

6.11. "Fans," pieced by Libby Shaifer Hollingsworth and John Montgomery, 1939–1943, set together and quilted by Dot Shaifer in 1982. Of all cotton materials, the quilt is hand-pieced and quilted by the piece and with a fan pattern in setting blocks. It is 74 inches wide by 84 inches long.

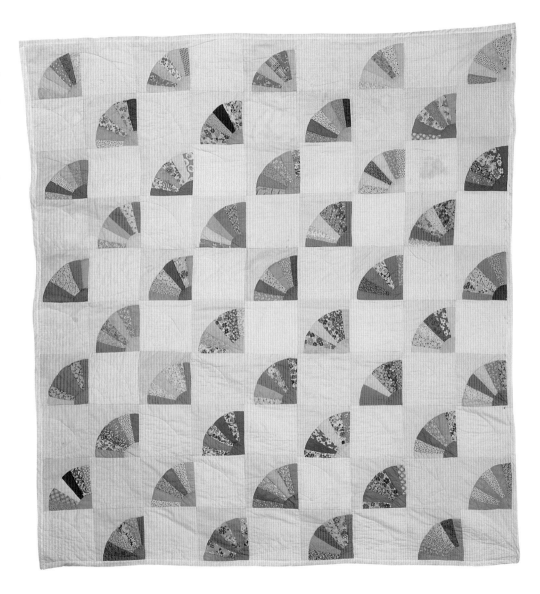

visit. In 1978, Dot and Shag moved to Port Gibson from their retirement in Arkansas in order to take care of Dear Laura and the house.

As Dot's daughter, Libby, was growing up, she saw all the women of her family—her mother, Grandmother Lizzie, Dear Laura, as well as other aunts and cousins—occupying themselves with some kind of needlework on a daily basis. In addition to the piecing and appliquéing and quilting of quilts, there was crocheting, needlepoint, knitting, and tatting going on all around Libby. She expected to eventually join in with what the grown-ups were doing.

However, needlework was not confined to the women. Libby's father, Shag, always worked on a needlepoint project during football and baseball games, whether listening to the radio, as he did in the beginning, or watching on television, which came later. He said his favorite pastime was "working on ladies' seats" (meaning chair bottoms). Libby remembers Shag, Dot, and Sammy working together in the 1940s to hook a nine-by-twelve-foot rug.

One of Libby's first projects was a fan quilt that she pieced in the late 1930s and early 1940s, beginning when she was seven years old and finishing when she was about ten. Her cousin, John Montgomery (the recipient of one of Lizzie's quilts), would occasionally help out, choosing and placing the colors of his fans as carefully as she did hers. It was forty years later that Dot came upon the little fan squares and set them together to be quilted.

Libby remembers that outside help would sometimes be called upon when quilt-making got a bit overwhelming for the Shaifer women. One woman, a Miss Nettie Sprott, would come to the house to help cut all the

6.12. "Home Sweet Home," cross-stitched kit quilt made by Dot Shaifer, c. 1961. Of all cotton materials, the quilt is quilted by pre-printed design at eight to nine stitches per inch. It is 81.5 inches wide by 93.5 inches long.

6.13. "Blue Delft," cross-stitched kit quilt made by Dot Shaifer, c. 1982. Of all cotton materials, the quilt is quilted by pre-printed design at nine stitches per inch. It is 81 inches wide by 93 inches long. It is one of a pair.

6.14. "Blue Leaves and Flowers," cross-stitched kit quilt made by Dot Shaifer and Laura Percy Shaifer, c. 1955. Of all cotton materials, the quilt is quilted by pre-printed design at nine stitches per inch. It is one of a pair.

6.15. "Red, Green, Blue, and Yellow," cross-stitched kit quilt made by Libby Shaifer Hollingsworth, c. 1961. Of all cotton materials, the quilt is quilted by pre-printed design at eight to nine stitches per inch. It is 80 inches wide by 94.5 inches long. It is one of a pair. Dot and Libby each made one.

6.16. "Central Medallion with Pomegranates," cross-stitched kit quilt made by Dot Shaifer and Libby Shaifer Hollingsworth, c. 1960. Of all cotton materials, the quilt is quilted by pre-printed design at nine stitches per inch. It is 78.5 inches wide by 92 inches long. It is one of a pair. Dot and Libby each made one.

6.17. "Cross-Stitched Ohio Rose," cross-stitched kit quilt made by Dot Shaifer and Laura Percy Shaifer, c. 1955. Of all cotton materials, the quilt is quilted by preprinted design at six to seven stitches per inch. It is 82 inches wide by 95 inches long. It is one of a pair.

6.18. Whole-cloth quilt, maker and date unknown. Of all cotton materials, it is hand-quilted at nine to ten stitches per inch, with prairie points used as edge finish. It is 65 inches wide by 93.5 inches long.

pieces needed for the quilts the Shaifers wanted to make. Miss Sprott would sometimes come back to help with the quilting. Quilts were sent out to be quilted from time to time—one bears a label that reads, "Quilted by Elise Bole." This outside help was needed over and above the quilting being done by the family, who never let up. This was an accepted practice of the day, one that in no way devalued the quilt; in fact, quilts to be entered into contests were regularly quilted by professional quilters rather than by the person whose name was on the entry.

6.19. Al and Libby Hollingsworth with grandson Tyler

From the late 1940s into the early 1960s, kit quilts that utilized cross-stitch to create the design of the top were about the only source of new and exciting designs, as interest in quilt patterns and kits had subsided across the nation and sales were down. Dot and Libby saw an excellent opportunity to combine their love of quilting with a new craft they had decided they enjoyed. From the late 1940s, when Libby was in her teens, through the next decade or so, they worked together to cross-stitch ten quilt kits, including four pairs of twin bed quilts. They usually sent their quilts out to church groups in the Mississippi Delta to be quilted. The reader may have noticed that the Shaifers never did believe in leaving a piece unfinished; there are only two unquilted tops in the entire collection—every other piece is quilted and bound.

Libby Hollingsworth has followed in the footsteps of her Shaifer forebears, establishing her own new family within the security and love of the old. Al, her husband, is an industrial engineer and was associated most of his professional life with Armstrong Rubber Company in New Haven,

Connecticut. When he retired in 1989, he was able to finally pursue his avocation of historic preservation, becoming manager of the Port Gibson Main Street, a program administered by the National Trust for Historic Preservation. Libby and Al moved in with her parents in the Church Street house, where they tended to her father until his death at ninety years of age. They remain very active in the communities in which they live, Port Gibson and Guilford, Connecticut, where they restored a two-hundred-year-old house.

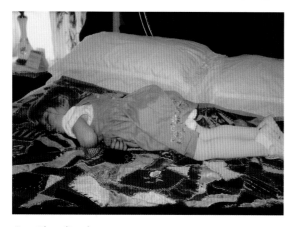

6.20. Threading the generations—Ashley Shaifer Moxey naps on her great-great-great-great grandparents wedding finery.

Libby devoted much of her creative time to crewel work when her three children were young because the projects were so much smaller than quilts. She seldom finds time to quilt today, having reached the point in her life where she is caring for her mother, enjoying her grandchildren, and, with her husband, working on various historic preservation projects.

Though she is not currently generating new pieces, Libby is participating in another very important aspect of quilting. The documentation and preservation of a collection such as the one for which Libby is caretaker requires a substantial amount of time, energy, research, and study. Libby Shaifer Hollingsworth does not take the responsibilities of ownership lightly and hopes to find or establish a place in which the public can enjoy her family's quilts for years to come.

NOTES

Chapter 1: The Back Story

1. Handwritten genealogy belonging to Elizabeth Shaifer Hollingsworth, prepared by unknown Shaifer ancestor, incorporating A. K. Shaifer Jr.'s recollections of his father, c. 1935 (hereafter cited as Shaifer genealogy).

2. Shaifer S. Carpenter, letter dated January 12, 1935, copy in collection of Elizabeth Shaifer Hollingsworth, Port Gibson, Mississippi.

3. Interview with Mrs. Kate Briscoe Shaifer Sholars, granddaughter of A. K. Shaifer, 1935, in handwritten genealogy.

4. Jonathan Daniels, *The Devil's Backbone: The Story of the Natchez Trace* (Gretna, LA: Pelican Publishing Company, 1998), 7.

5. Many houses in Port Gibson were built from the timber of flatboats that had made their way to their destination on Bayou Pierre, which flanks Port Gibson on the north. When the water in Bayou Pierre was high enough, steamboats could also make the passage in from the Mississippi River to pick up passengers and cargo; the traffic on the bayou was never as heavy as on the river, where regular stops were made at Grand Gulf and Bruinsburg. See Mary H. Ellis, *Cannonballs and Courage: The Story of Port Gibson* (Virginia Beach, VA: Donning Company Publishers, 2003), 34, 43.

6. Shaifer genealogy.

7. Letter of Percy Leon Shaifer, dated August 17, 1935, copy in collection of Elizabeth Shaifer Hollingsworth, Port Gibson, Mississippi.

8. Shaifer genealogy.

9. Libby Shaifer Hollingsworth, "Shaifer House and Port Gibson Battlefield," manuscript, given as testimony before the Congressional Civil War Commission, March 27, 1998.

10. Mary Elizabeth Johnson, *Mississippi Quilts* (Jackson: University Press of Mississippi, 2001).

11. Claiborne County Record of Probate, vol. 1862–1869, 258, Port Gibson, Mississippi.

12. Carol Vickers's interview with Libby Shaifer Hollingsworth, c. May 15, 1997, Port Gibson, Mississippi.

13. Shaifer genealogy.

Chapter 2: The Battle of Port Gibson

1. Shaifer genealogy.

2. Hollingsworth, "Shaifer House and Port Gibson Battlefield," quote from the *Fontanello, Iowa, Observer,* reprinted in the *Port Gibson Reveille,* May 9, 1907.

3. Ellis, *Cannonballs and Courage,* 63.

4. Hollingsworth, "Shaifer House and Port Gibson Battlefield," 1998.

5. State historic marker in front of A. K. Shaifer house.

6. Ellis, *Cannonballs and Courage,* 67.

7. Daniels, *The Devil's Backbone,* 261.

8. Hollingsworth, "Shaifer House and Port Gibson Battlefield," 1998.

Chapter 3: After the War

1. Spooner Forbes's 1872 diary, in possession of Mississippi Department of Archives and History, Jackson, Mississippi.

2. Ibid.

Chapter 4: Unique New Friendships

1. Shaifer genealogy.

2. Kell Shaifer, letter to Reuben Hart, May 27, 1912, copy in collection of Elizabeth Shaifer Hollingsworth, Port Gibson, Mississippi.

3. Kell Shaifer, memorial to William Duffner, in the *Mitchell (IN) Commercial,* December 21, 1913.

4. Girault McArthur Jones, *That Reminds Me: A Memoir* (Sewanee, TN: University of the South, 1984), 16–17.

Chapter 5: Mother and Daughter

1. Ellis, *Cannonballs and Courage,* 94.

2. Johnson, *Mississippi Quilts.*

3. According to Thos. K. Woodard and Blanche Greenstein, in *Twentieth Century Quilts: 1900–1950* (New York: E. P. Dutton, 1988), 12: "The first two pattern catalogues, those published by the Ladies Art Company in 1898 and by Clara Stone in 1910, were devoted almost entirely to traditional designs from the nineteenth century and are welcome references today. Their research provided the foundation for many of the pattern catalogues that were to follow."

4. Roderick Kiracofe and Mary Elizabeth Johnson, *The American Quilt: A History of Cloth and Comfort, 1750–1950* (New York: Clarkson N. Potter, 2004), 247.

5. Woodard and Greenstein, *Twentieth Century Quilts,* 11.

6. Barbara Brackman, *An Encyclopedia of Pieced Quilt Patterns* (Lawrence, KS: Prairie Flower Publishing, 1984), 3:170.

Chapter 6: Into the Twenty-First Century

1. Woodard and Greenstein, *Twentieth Century Quilts,* 10.

2. Ibid., 20.

3. Merikay Waldvogel and Barbara Brackman, *Patchwork Souvenirs of the 1933 World's Fair* (Nashville: Rutledge Hill Press, 1993), 42.

BIBLIOGRAPHY

Brackman, Barbara. *An Encyclopedia of Pieced Quilt Patterns.* Vols. 1–8. Lawrence, KS: Prairie Flower Publishing, 1984.

Carpenter, Shaifer S. Letter dated January 12, 1935. Copy in collection of Elizabeth Shaifer Hollingsworth, Port Gibson, Mississippi.

Claiborne County Record of Probate. Vol. 1862–1869, Port Gibson, Mississippi.

Daniels, Jonathan. *The Devil's Backbone: The Story of the Natchez Trace.* Gretna, LA: Pelican Publishing Company, 1998.

Ellis, Mary H. *Cannonballs and Courage: The Story of Port Gibson.* Virginia Beach, VA: Donning Company Publishers, 2003.

Forbes, Spooner. Personal diary, 1872. Private collection in possession of Mississippi Department of Archives and History, Jackson, Mississippi.

Hollingsworth, Elizabeth "Libby" Shaifer. "Shaifer House and Port Gibson Battlefield." Undated manuscript in possession of author.

Johnson, Mary Elizabeth. Interview with Elizabeth "Libby" Shaifer Hollingsworth, September 17, 2002, Port Gibson, Mississippi.

Johnson, Mary Elizabeth. *Mississippi Quilts.* Jackson: University Press of Mississippi, 2001.

Jones, Girault McArthur. *That Reminds Me: A Memoir.* Sewanee, TN: University of the South, 1984.

Kiracofe, Roderick, and Mary Elizabeth Johnson. *The American Quilt: A History of Cloth and Comfort, 1750–1950.* New York: Clarkson N. Potter, 1993 and 2004.

Shaifer ancestor. Handwritten genealogy belonging to Elizabeth Shaifer Hollingsworth. Prepared by unknown Shaifer ancestor, incorporating A. K. Shaifer Jr.'s recollections of his father, c. 1940.

Shaifer, Percy Leon. Letter dated August 17, 1935. Copy in collection of Elizabeth Shaifer Hollingsworth, Port Gibson, Mississippi.

State historic marker in front of A. K. Shaifer house, west of Port Gibson, Mississippi.

Trestain, Eileen Jahnke. *Dating Fabrics: A Color Guide, 1800–1960.* Paducah, KY: American Quilter's Society, 1998.

Vickers, Carol. Interview with Elizabeth "Libby" Shaifer Hollingsworth, c. May 17, 1997, Port Gibson, Mississippi.

Waldvogel, Merikay, and Barbara Brackman. *Patchwork Souvenirs of the 1933 World's Fair.* Nashville: Rutledge Hill Press, 1993.

Woodard, Thos. K., and Blache Greenstein. *Twentieth-Century Quilts: 1900–1950.* New York: E. P. Dutton, 1988.

INDEX

References to illustrations appear in **boldface**.

Armstrong Rubber Co., 107
art deco, 92
art nouveau, 92

Baker, Virginia Brown, 88, **88**
Baker, Joseph Holmes, 88, **88**, 90
Bayou Pierre, 17
Beauvoir (Orange Grove), **88**
Blakely, Battle of, 31
Bole, Elise, 107
Butler, Zebulon, 29

Cabot, Nancy, 67
Chicago Tribune, 67
Civil War, 21, 23, **31**, **37**. *See also specific battles*
Claranook Plantation, 23
comforts, 20

Davis, Jefferson, 23, **88**

Decoration Day, 44–45. *See also* Memorial Day
Dorsey, Sarah Ann, 88
Duffner, William, 42, 48

Fayette, Miss., 16
flatboats, 15
Forbes, Spooner, 31, 40, 42, **42**

Good Housekeeping Magazine, 67
Grand Gulf Military Park Museum, 46
Grant, Ulysses S., 26, 29
Greenstein, Blanche, 93
Grindstone Ford, 17

Hart, Reuben, 45
Hollingsworth, Al, 87, 107–8, **107**
Hollingsworth, Elizabeth (Libby) Shaifer, 9, 10, 60, 87, **97**, 99, **103**, **104**, **107**, 108
Holly Hill, 8, 9, 19, 20, **20**, 21, 23, 25, 27, 31, 42, 45, 48, 51
Houston, Sam, 14–15

Humphreys, Elizabeth Hannah, 17
Humphreys, George Wilson, 17
Humphreys, General Ralph, 17

Jones, Ben Shaifer, **82**
Jones, Girault McArthur, 51

Magnolia Church, Battle of, 26, 27, 30
Mammy Mary, 28, **29**
McCall's Pattern Co., 67
McClernand, General John A., 27
Memorial Day, 45, 52. *See also*
        Decoration Day
Mississippi Quilt Association, 9
Mississippi Quilts, 60
Montgomery, John, **98**, 99
Moxey, Tyler Andrew, **107**

Natchez Trace, 7, 15, 16
National Trust for Historic
        Preservation, 108
New Orleans, La., 15–16

Orr, Ann, 67

Parrish, Maxfield, 92
Port Gibson, Battle of, 25, 29, 44
Port Gibson Oil Works, 53
Port Gibson Reveille, 51

quilt kits, 83, 93, 107
quilt pattern, designers. *See* Cabot,
        Nancy; Orr, Ann; Parrish,
        Maxfield
quilt patterns
  appliqué
    Broderie perse, 21
    Butterfly, **82**, 84
    Colonial rose, 97
    Crossed tulips, **76**
    Dresden plate (dessert plate), 68,
        74, 83, 85
    Floral basket, 69, **72**
    Iris, **91**, 92, 97
    Ice cream cone, 83
    Ohio rose, **95**, 97
    Old fashioned spray, 69, **71**
    Pink dogwood, **96**, 97
    Poinsettia, **94**, 97
    Pomegranate, 40, **41**
    Shamrock, **70**
    Triple tulips, **68**, 69, **75**, 85
  pieced (patchwork)
    Album cross, 55, **59**
    All hands round, **32**, 34
    Baseball, **33**
    Basket weave, **78**
    Churn dash, **43**
    Circle, **33**

Corn and beans, 34, **37**

Double Irish chain, **79**, **82**, 85

Double nine patch (H block), 66, **66**, 68

Double wedding ring, **73**, 83, 85

Dove at the window, 55, 58

Drunkard's path, **62**, 64, 67

Fans, 98

Gardener's prize, 64

Grandmother's flower garden, **80**, 85

Kit quilt, **72**, **100**

Log cabin (courthouse steps), 46, **47**, 51

Log cabin (straight furrows), 34, **36**, 46

Nine patch, 34, **35**, 55, **56**

Ocean waves, 34, **39**, 55

Pinwheel, 34, **38**, 55, 64, 65

Rob Peter to pay Paul, 64

Snowball wreath, 67

Stove eye, **33**, 34, 55

String, **49**, 50

This and that, **57**

Whirling star, **81**, 86

crosstitch kit

   Baltimore album, **103**

   Blue delft, **101**

   Blue leaves and flowers, **102**

   Central medallion with pome-granates, **104**

   Home sweet home, **100**

   Ohio rose, **105**

   whole cloth, 28, **28**, 106

quilter, professional. *See* Bole, Elise; Sprott, Nettie

quilting patterns

   "Baptist fan," **32**, **37**, **43**, **56**, **78**

   by-the-piece, **36**, **39**, **41**, **61**, **68**, **74**, **76**, **77**, **78**, **81**, **84**, **94**, **95**, **98**

   crosshatch, **38**, **75**, **94**

   diagonal, **57**

   feathered wreath, **86**

   floral design, **95**

   machine, **47**

   overall grid, **79**, **82**

   preprinted design, **100**, **101**, **102**, 103, **104**, **105**

Schaeffer, Elizabeth Keller, 13

Schaeffer, Henry, 13, 14

Sears Quilt Contest, 93

Shaifer, Abram Keller, 7, 8, 9, 13–19, 21, 22, 23, **82**

Shaifer, Abram Keller (Kell), Jr., 13, 16, 19, 24, **25**, 31, 44, **48**, 51, 52

Shaifer, Abram Keller, III, 25, 29, 31, 51

Shaifer, Abram Keller, IV, 60, **97**

Shaifer, Amanda Guice, 31, **31**, 34, 40, 42, 46, 48, **48**, **49**, 50, **51**, 55

Shaifer, Benjamin Humphreys, 25, 29, 31, 51

Shaifer, Dorothy Davidson, **54**, 87, 88, 90, **90**, **91**, **94**, **95**, **96**, 97, **97**, **98**, 100, 101, **102**, 104, 105

Shaifer, Edgar D., **54**, 55

Shaifer, Edwin Thomas, 30

Shaifer, Elizabeth Chamberlain Girault, 24, 25, **25**, 27, 30

Shaifer, Elizabeth Estelle, 55

Shaifer, Elizabeth Hannah Humphreys (Betsey), **18**, 19, 20, 21, 22, 23, 29, 40

Shaifer, Elizabeth Wheeless (Lizzie), 53, **54**, **56**, **57**, **58**, **59**, **61**, **62**, **63**, 65, **65**, **68**, 68, 69, **70**, **71**, **72**, **73**, 74, 77, 79, 83, **84**, 86, 87, **91**, **94**, 99

Shaifer, George Girault, 26

Shaifer, Laura Percy (Dear Laura), 55, 60, **60**, 65, 69, **75**, **76**, 77, 78, **80**, **81**, 83, 85, 86, 87, **91**, **94**, **97**, 99, **102**, **105**

Shaifer, Mary, **8**

Shaifer, Percy Leon, 31, 42, 51, 53, **54**, 65

Shaifer, Sanfrid Blomquist (Shag), **54**, 60, 87, 97, **97**, 99

Shaifer, Sanfrid Davidson (Sammy), 87

Shaifer, Stephen Pillsworth (Dr. Pill), 23, 24

Sprott, Nettie, 99

Stearns & Foster (Mountain Mist), 94, 95

Tellie's Garrison, 14

toile, 21

veterans
    Confederate, 46
    Union, 42, 44, 46

Vicksburg, Battle of, 29, 46

Wheeless, Elizabeth, 40, 42, 51

Wheeless, Martha, 40

Wheeless, Mary Jane, 40, 42, **42**

Wheeless, Sally, 40

Women's Christian Temperance Union, 90

Woodard, Thomas K., 93

World War I, effect on quilting, 65

yellow fever, 42, 51